HAMLYN'S ALL-COLOUR BOOK OF

Soups and Starters

HAMLYN

LONDON · NEW YORK · SYDNEY · TORONTO

Acknowledgements
Recipes created by Rosemary Wadey
Photography by John Lee
Cover picture by Iain Reid
Artwork by John Scott Martin
China kindly loaned by Josiah Wedgwood and Sons Limited

Published by
The Hamlyn Publishing Group Limited
London · New York · Sydney · Toronto
Astronaut House, Feltham, Middlesex, England
© Copyright The Hamlyn Publishing Group Limited 1977
ISBN 0 600 38229 X

Printed in England by Jarrold and Sons Limited, Norwich

Contents

Introduction

Soups and starters play an important role in a menu, whether for a dinner party, a simple family meal or for a special occasion, as they introduce the food that is to follow. Neither should be too highly flavoured or too filling.

The recipes have been selected to cater for the needs of today's cook and to give some new ideas. There are many kinds of soups – thin and clear, thick and creamy, hot or cold. Remember that a thin soup should be served with a hearty main course and a thicker soup as the starter to a light steak and salad main course. Soups can also be served as a lunch or snack with French bread. Cold soups make a refreshing dish to serve on a warm summer's day.

To give soups eye appeal, always garnish them. Try a sprinkling of grated cheese, chopped fresh herbs, croûtons or a swirl of cream or natural yogurt which adds the final touch of sophistication.

The starter recipes include many new ways with salads, vegetables, fruit, pâtés, eggs and cheese, fish and celebration starters such as seafood bouchées. Textures, flavours and colours have been combined to make an exciting beginning to your meals. There are some starters which, when in season, are reasonably priced – for example avocado pears, asparagus, grapefruit, melon and fish.

The starter to a meal should be selected to contrast with the food which is to follow. For example if you plan to serve fish as a main course, do not choose a fish starter. Bear in mind the flavour, colour and texture of your menu so that all dishes give a balance and create the right atmosphere for your family and guests to enjoy the food.

Soups and starters freezing facts

Soups Most soups freeze well. Pour the cooled soup into freezer foil bags, rigid polythene containers or a polythene bag placed inside a rigid container, leaving a headspace in each case. Seal and label. Keep for 4–6 months.

To serve, allow to thaw and reheat slowly, bringing to the boil.

With soups containing cream, egg yolks or a garnish, add just before serving.

Starters With salad and vegetable starters: the salad vegetables do not freeze but most other vegetables freeze well providing they are blanched first. Pâtés are excellent freezer candidates. Cook and freeze them in a foil dish or, when cold, turn out and wrap in a double layer of foil. Before serving, allow to thaw at room temperature.

Bouchée cases may be baked and frozen. Prepare the filling separately and spoon the hot filling into the reheated cases. Quiches may also be baked and frozen. Defrost and heat through in a moderate oven.

Useful facts and figures

Notes on metrication

In this book quantities are given in metric, imperial and American measures. Exact conversion from imperial to metric measures does not usually give very convenient working quantities and so the metric measures have been rounded off into units of 25 grams. The table below shows the recommended equivalents.

Ounces	Approx. g to nearest whole figure	Recommended conversion to nearest unit of 25
1	28	25
2	57	50
3	85	75
4	113	100
5	142	150
6	170	175
7	198	200
8	227	225
9	255	250
10	283	275
11	312	300
12	340	350
13	368	375
14	397	400
15	425	425
16 (1 lb)	454	450
17	482	475
18	510	500
19	539	550
20	567	575

Note: When converting quantities over 20 oz first add the appropriate figures in the centre column, then adjust to the nearest unit of 25. As a general guide, 1 kg (1000 g) equals 2.2 lb or about 2 lb 3 oz. This method of conversion gives good results in nearly all cases but in certain pastry recipes a more accurate conversion is necessary to produce a balanced recipe. On the other hand, quantities of such ingredients as vegetables, fruit, meat and fish which are not critical are rounded off to the nearest quarter of a kg as this is how they are likely to be purchased.

Liquid measures The millilitre has been used in this book and the following table gives a few examples:

Imperial	Approx. ml to nearest whole figure	Recommended ml
$\frac{1}{4}$ pint	142	150 ml
$\frac{1}{2}$ pint	283	300 ml
$\frac{3}{4}$ pint	425	450 ml
1 pint	567	600 ml
$1\frac{1}{2}$ pints	851	900 ml
$1\frac{3}{4}$ pints	992	1000 ml (1 litre)

Note: For quantities of $1\frac{3}{4}$ pints and over we have used litres and fractions of a litre.

Spoon measures All spoon measures given in this book are level.

Can sizes At present, cans are marked with the exact (usually to the nearest whole number) metric equivalent of the imperial weight of the contents, so we have followed this practice when giving can sizes.

Oven temperatures

The table below gives recommended equivalents.

	°F	°C	Gas Mark
Very cool	225	110	$\frac{1}{4}$
	250	120	$\frac{1}{2}$
Cool	275	140	1
	300	150	2
Moderate	325	160	3
	350	180	4
Moderately hot	375	190	5
	400	200	6
Hot	425	220	7
	450	230	8
Very hot	475	240	9

Note: When making any of the recipes in this book, only follow one set of measures as they are not interchangeable.

Notes for American users

Although the recipes in this book give American measures, the lists below give some equivalents or substitutes for terms and commodities which may be unfamiliar to American readers.

Equipment and terms
BRITISH/AMERICAN

cocktail stick/toothpick
frying pan/skillet
greaseproof paper/wax paper
grill/broil
kitchen paper/paper towels
liquidise/blend
mince/grind
packet/package
polythene/plastic
stoned/pitted

Ingredients
BRITISH/AMERICAN

aubergine/eggplant
beetroot/beet
black olives/ripe olives
boiling fowl/stewing chicken
chicory/Belgian endive
cooking apple/baking apple
cornflour/cornstarch
courgettes/zucchini
double cream/heavy cream
gelatine/gelatin
gherkin/sweet dill pickle
ham/cured or smoked ham
haricot beans/navy beans
natural yogurt/unflavored yogurt
shortcrust pastry/basic pie dough
single cream/light cream
spring onions/scallions
sticks celery/stalks celery
streaky bacon rashers/bacon slices
sultanas/seedless white raisins
sweetcorn/corn kernels
tomato ketchup/tomato catsup
tomato purée/tomato paste
top of the milk/half and half
unsalted butter/sweet butter

Note: The British and Australian pint is 20 fluid ounces as opposed to the American pint which is 16 fluid ounces.

Notes for Australian users

Ingredients in this book are given in cup, metric and imperial measures. In Australia the American 8-oz measuring cup is used in conjunction with the Imperial pint of 20 fluid ounces. It is most important to remember that the Australian tablespoon differs from both the British and American tablespoons; the table below gives a comparison between the standard tablespoons used in the three countries. The British standard tablespoon holds 17.7 millilitres, the American 14.2 millilitres, and the Australian 20 millilitres. A teaspoon holds approximately 5 millilitres in all three countries.

British	American	Australian
1 teaspoon	1 teaspoon	1 teaspoon
1 tablespoon	1 tablespoon	1 tablespoon
2 tablespoons	3 tablespoons	2 tablespoons
$3\frac{1}{2}$ tablespoons	4 tablespoons	3 tablespoons
4 tablespoons	5 tablespoons	$3\frac{1}{2}$ tablespoons

Hot soups

What could be more warming on a cold winter's day than a bowl of hot soup? Home-made soup is a good choice for a starter to a light main course; soup can also be served with slices of hot crusty French bread as a midday snack or late supper dish.

Minestrone soup

METRIC/IMPERIAL/AMERICAN
50 g/2 oz/⅓ cup haricot beans
1.75 litres/3 pints/7½ cups stock
2 carrots, chopped
1 large onion, chopped
1 clove garlic, crushed
2 leeks, trimmed, thinly sliced and washed
3 tablespoons/3 tablespoons/¼ cup oil
25 g/1 oz/2 tablespoons butter
1 (396-g/14-oz/14-oz) can peeled tomatoes
1 tablespoon tomato purée
bouquet garni
salt and pepper
50 g/2 oz/¼ cup spaghetti, broken up
Parmesan cheese

Soak the beans in 600 ml/1 pint/2½ cups of the stock overnight. The following day add a further 600 ml/1 pint/2½ cups stock and simmer gently for 1 hour.

Fry the carrot, onion, garlic and leeks in a mixture of oil and butter until soft – about 5 minutes – and until just beginning to colour. Add the remaining ingredients (except the spaghetti and cheese), the beans, all the stock and bring to the boil. Cover and simmer gently for 1 hour or until tender. Add the spaghetti and continue cooking for 10–15 minutes until tender. Discard the bouquet garni, adjust the seasoning and serve sprinkled with Parmesan cheese.

Serves 4–6

Kidney soup

METRIC/IMPERIAL/AMERICAN
225 g/8 oz/½ lb ox kidney, skinned, cored and chopped
25 g/1 oz/¼ cup seasoned flour
1 large onion, finely chopped
40 g/1½ oz/3 tablespoons dripping or butter
generous litre/2 pints/5 cups beef stock
bouquet garni
salt and pepper
dash Worcestershire sauce
1 teaspoon tomato purée
HERB DUMPLINGS:
100 g/4 oz/1 cup self-raising flour
50 g/2 oz/½ cup shredded suet
1 teaspoon mixed herbs

Toss the kidney in the seasoned flour. Fry with the onion in the dripping for about 5 minutes until beginning to brown, stirring. Stir in the remaining flour and the stock. Add the bouquet garni and bring to the boil. Cover and simmer for about 1 hour.

Remove the bouquet garni and sieve or liquidise the soup. Return to the pan. Adjust the seasoning, add the Worcestershire sauce and tomato purée. Bring to the boil for 2 minutes and serve with the dumplings.

To make the dumplings, mix the flour with the shredded suet, seasoning and herbs. Add sufficient water to mix to an elastic dough. Form into 12 balls and simmer gently in boiling salted water for 15 minutes. Drain and add to the soup.

Serves 4–6

Carrot soup

METRIC/IMPERIAL/AMERICAN
0.5 kg/1 lb/1 lb carrots, sliced
2 sticks celery, chopped
1 large onion, chopped
25 g/1 oz/2 tablespoons butter
1 tablespoon oil
750 ml/1¼ pints/3 cups stock
1 bay leaf
grated rind and juice of ½ orange
1 tablespoon lemon juice
salt and pepper
150 ml/¼ pint/⅔ cup single cream
chopped chives to garnish

Fry the carrot, celery and onion gently in the butter and oil for 5–10 minutes, stirring occasionally. Add the stock, bay leaf, orange rind and juice, lemon juice and seasoning. Bring to the boil, cover and simmer gently for 25–30 minutes. Remove the bay leaf, sieve or liquidise the soup and return to the pan. Add the cream, adjust the seasoning and bring just up to the boil. Serve sprinkled with chives.

Serves 4–6

Cock-a-leekie soup

METRIC/IMPERIAL/AMERICAN
1 (1.25–1.5-kg/2½–3-lb/2½–3-lb) oven-ready boiling fowl
1.5–2.25 litres/3–4 pints/7½–10 cups water or stock
4 leeks, trimmed, thinly sliced and washed
salt and pepper
bouquet garni
12 prunes, soaked overnight

Truss the bird and place in a large pan with the washed giblets (if available), water or stock, leeks, seasoning and bouquet garni. Bring to the boil and remove the scum. Cover and simmer gently for 2½–3 hours until the bird is tender. Add the prunes and continue cooking for about 20 minutes.

Remove the bouquet garni and the bird. Spoon off any fat from the soup. Chop some of the chicken flesh and return it to the soup. Adjust the seasoning and serve with hot crusty bread.
Note: The remainder of the chicken can be used in a pie or other dish.

Serves 6–8

Mulligatawny soup

METRIC/IMPERIAL/AMERICAN
1 large onion, chopped
2 carrots, chopped
225 g/8 oz/1⅓ cups tomatoes, peeled and chopped
3 sticks celery, chopped
1 apple, peeled, cored and chopped
50 g/2 oz/¼ cup dripping
2 tablespoons/2 tablespoons/3 tablespoons flour
2–4 teaspoons curry powder
generous litre/2 pints/5 cups beef stock
salt and pepper
100 g/4 oz/½ cup left-over cooked beef or lamb, minced
50 g/2 oz/⅓ cup cooked rice
chopped parsley to garnish

Fry the vegetables and apple in the dripping until soft and beginning to colour. Stir in the flour and curry powder and cook for 1 minute. Add the stock and seasoning. Bring to the boil, cover and simmer for about 1½ hours, stirring occasionally.

Sieve or liquidise the soup and return to the pan. Add the minced meat and cooked rice. Bring back to the boil for 2–3 minutes, adjust the seasoning and serve sprinkled with parsley.

Serves 6

Cream of onion soup

METRIC/IMPERIAL/AMERICAN
50 g/2 oz/¼ cup butter
350 g/12 oz/3 cups onions, finely chopped
2 sticks celery, finely chopped
900 ml/1½ pints/3¾ cups chicken stock
1 blade mace
1 bay leaf
salt and pepper
25 g/1 oz/¼ cup flour
150 ml/¼ pint/⅔ cup milk
150 ml/¼ pint/⅔ cup single or double cream
GARNISH:
fried croûtons
chopped fresh mixed herbs

Melt the butter in a pan and fry the onion and celery for
5 minutes without browning. Add the stock, mace, bay leaf and
seasoning. Bring to the boil, cover and simmer for about 45
minutes or until tender. Remove the bay leaf and mace. The
soup can be sieved or liquidised if a smooth soup is preferred.

Blend the flour with the milk and whisk gradually into the
soup. Return to the boil, stirring continuously, and simmer for
5 minutes. Adjust the seasoning, stir in the cream and reheat
before serving. Dip the hot fried croûtons into finely chopped
mixed herbs and float them on top of the soup.

Serves 4–6

Consommé

METRIC/IMPERIAL/AMERICAN
generous litre/2 pints/5 cups good beef stock
175 g/6 oz/¾ cup lean beef, minced
2 tablespoons/2 tablespoons/3 tablespoons tomato pulp
   (optional)
1 carrot, chopped
1 small onion, quartered
bouquet garni
whites and shells of 2 eggs
salt and pepper
1 tablespoon sherry (optional)
few julienne strips of cooked carrot

Place the stock in a pan with the beef and leave to soak for
1 hour. Add the tomato, carrot, onion, bouquet garni, unbeaten
egg whites, crushed shells and plenty of seasoning. Whisk until
nearly boiling then bring to the boil. Simmer very gently for
1 hour, taking care not to break the frothy layer on top.

Pour through a jelly bag or scalded cloth, keeping the froth
back until last. Then pour through the filter of egg in the cloth
again. Return to the pan, adjusting the seasoning if necessary
but take care not to cloud the soup. A little sherry can be added,
if liked. Place the cooked julienne strips of carrot into the
consommé. Serve with breadsticks.

Serves 4

Leek and potato soup

METRIC/IMPERIAL/AMERICAN
3 leeks, trimmed, sliced and washed
1 onion, sliced
350 g/12 oz/2 cups potatoes, peeled and chopped
40 g/1½ oz/3 tablespoons dripping
generous litre/2 pints/5 cups chicken stock
2 large carrots
salt and pepper
ground nutmeg

Fry the prepared vegetables gently in the dripping until soft but not coloured. Add the stock, whole carrots and seasoning, and bring to the boil. Cover and simmer gently until very tender – about 30 minutes.

Remove the carrots and cut into dice. Sieve or liquidise the soup and return to the pan. Adjust the seasoning and add the nutmeg to taste. Add the diced carrots to the soup, simmer for 2–3 minutes and serve sprinkled with a little more nutmeg if liked.

Serves 6

Tomato and orange soup

METRIC/IMPERIAL/AMERICAN
1 stick celery, chopped
1 onion, chopped
1 carrot, chopped
2 rashers bacon, derinded and chopped
25 g/1 oz/2 tablespoons butter or dripping
2 tablespoons/2 tablespoons/3 tablespoons flour
1 tablespoon tomato purée
0.5 kg/1 lb/2½ cups tomatoes, peeled and chopped
900 ml/1½ pints/3¾ cups stock
salt and pepper
bouquet garni
sugar to taste
1 large orange
GARNISH:
single cream
slices of orange

Sauté the vegetables and bacon in the butter for 5 minutes until beginning to brown. Stir in the flour and tomato purée. Add the tomatoes, stock, seasoning and bouquet garni, and bring to the boil. Cover and simmer gently for about 40 minutes.

Remove the bouquet garni and sieve or liquidise the soup. Return to the pan, add a pinch of sugar and the grated rind and juice of the orange. Bring back to the boil for 2 minutes and adjust the seasoning. Garnish each bowl of soup with a swirl of cream and a quartered slice of orange.
Note: Canned tomatoes can be used in place of the fresh ones.

Serves 6

Cream of mushroom soup

METRIC/IMPERIAL/AMERICAN
1 large onion, finely chopped
1 clove garlic, crushed
75 g/3 oz/6 tablespoons butter
350 g/12 oz/3 cups button mushrooms
50 g/2 oz/$\frac{1}{2}$ cup flour
600 ml/1 pint/$2\frac{1}{2}$ cups chicken stock
salt and pepper
good pinch ground mace
600 ml/1 pint/$2\frac{1}{2}$ cups milk
1–2 teaspoons lemon juice
150 ml/$\frac{1}{4}$ pint/$\frac{2}{3}$ cup single cream
fried onion rings to garnish

Fry the onion and garlic in the butter until soft. Roughly chop half the mushrooms, add to the pan and fry gently until soft. Stir in the flour until well mixed then gradually add the stock and bring to the boil. Season well, add the mace; cover and simmer for 15–20 minutes.

Sieve or liquidise the soup and return to the pan. Finely chop the remaining mushrooms and add to the soup together with the milk. Bring back to the boil and simmer for 10 minutes. Add the lemon juice and cream, and reheat – do not boil. Garnish with crisply fried onion rings.

Serves 6

French onion soup

METRIC/IMPERIAL/AMERICAN
0.5 kg/1 lb/1 lb onions, very thinly sliced
65 g/$2\frac{1}{2}$ oz/5 tablespoons butter
1 tablespoon flour
scant 1.5 litres/$2\frac{1}{2}$ pints/$6\frac{1}{4}$ cups beef stock
salt and black pepper
2 bay leaves
6 slices French bread
75 g/3 oz/$\frac{3}{4}$ cup Cheddar cheese, finely grated

Fry the onions gently in the melted butter until evenly browned all over, stirring frequently to prevent any pieces from burning. Stir in the flour then gradually add the stock and bring up to the boil. Season well and add the bay leaves. Cover and simmer for about 30 minutes. Remove the bay leaves from the soup and adjust the seasoning.

Lay the slices of bread on a baking sheet and cover with grated cheese. Allow the cheese to just melt under a warm grill. Ladle the soup into bowls and serve with the bread slices floating on top.

Serves 6   *Illustrated on the cover*

Mixed fish chowder

METRIC/IMPERIAL/AMERICAN
2 rashers lean bacon, derinded and chopped
1 onion, finely sliced
25 g/1 oz/2 tablespoons butter
1 (396-g/14-oz/14-oz) can peeled tomatoes
750 ml/1¼ pints/3 cups fish stock
1 bay leaf
salt and pepper
50 g/2 oz/⅓ cup long-grain rice
225 g/8 oz/½ lb cooked haddock or cod, flaked
100 g/4 oz/⅔ cup peeled prawns
1 tablespoon chopped parsley
2 tablespoons/2 tablespoons/3 tablespoons cream
few whole prawns to garnish

Fry the bacon and onion in the butter until beginning to colour.
Add the tomatoes, stock, bay leaf, seasoning and rice. Bring to
the boil, cover and simmer for 20 minutes or until the rice is
cooked, stirring occasionally. Add the fish and prawns and
continue cooking for 10 minutes. Remove the bay leaf. Adjust
the seasoning, stir in the parsley and cream, and serve garnished
with the whole prawns.

Serves 4–6

Oatmeal and vegetable soup

METRIC/IMPERIAL/AMERICAN
50 g/2 oz/¼ cup dripping or butter
1 large onion, finely chopped
1 turnip, finely chopped
2 large carrots, chopped
1 large leek, trimmed, thinly sliced and washed
25 g/1 oz/⅓ cup medium oatmeal
900 ml/1½ pints/3¾ cups stock
salt and black pepper
450 ml/¾ pint/2 cups milk

Melt the fat in a pan and sauté all the vegetables for about
5 minutes without browning. Stir in the oatmeal and continue
cooking for a few minutes, stirring frequently. Add the stock
and seasoning, and bring to the boil. Cover and simmer for
about 1 hour or until all the vegetables are tender.

Add the milk, adjust the seasoning and bring back to the boil
for 3–4 minutes. Serve piping hot.

Serves 4–6

Mussel and onion soup

METRIC/IMPERIAL/AMERICAN
2.25 litres/4 pints/5 pints mussels
½ bottle dry white wine
2 large onions, finely chopped
50 g/2 oz/¼ cup butter
50 g/2 oz/½ cup flour
1 litre/1¾ pints/4¼ cups milk
salt and pepper
1 tablespoon lemon juice
2 tablespoons/2 tablespoons/3 tablespoons chopped
    parsley
150 ml/¼ pint/⅔ cup cream

Wash and scrub the mussels thoroughly, discarding any that are
open or that do not close when given a sharp tap. Place in a pan
with the wine and onions. Bring to the boil, cover and simmer
very gently for about 10 minutes until all the mussels are open.
Remove the mussels and take most of them out of their shells,
reserving a few mussels in half shells to garnish.

Melt the butter in a pan and stir in the flour. Cook for
1 minute then gradually add the mussel liquor followed by the
milk. Bring to the boil, stirring frequently, season to taste and
sharpen with lemon juice. Simmer for 5 minutes. Add the
mussels and continue cooking for 2–3 minutes. Stir in the
parsley and cream, and reheat without boiling. Garnish with the
reserved mussels. Serve with hot crusty French bread.

Serves 6

Giblet soup

METRIC/IMPERIAL/AMERICAN
0.5 kg/1 lb/1 lb giblets
2 onions, chopped
2 sticks celery, chopped
2 carrots, chopped
salt and pepper
1.5 litres/2½ pints/6¼ cups stock or water
1 bay leaf
25–50 g/1–2 oz/about ⅓ cup long-grain rice
2 carrots, coarsely grated
GARNISH:
chopped parsley
fried croûtons

Wash the giblets thoroughly, discarding any yellow parts on the
gizzard and liver. Place in a pan with the onion, celery, carrot,
seasoning, stock and bay leaf. Bring to the boil. Skim, cover and
simmer for 2 hours.

Strain and return the soup to the pan with the rice, grated
carrot and some of the finely chopped giblet meat. The cooked
vegetables can be sieved or liquidised and added to the soup.
Simmer for a further 20 minutes, adjust the seasoning and
garnish with the parsley and fried croûtons of bread.

Serves 6

Creamed corn soup

METRIC/IMPERIAL/AMERICAN
50 g/2 oz/$\frac{1}{4}$ cup butter
1 tablespoon chopped onion
40 g/1$\frac{1}{2}$ oz/6 tablespoons flour
1 teaspoon curry powder
1 tablespoon tomato purée
600 ml/1 pint/2$\frac{1}{2}$ cups stock
300 ml/$\frac{1}{2}$ pint/1$\frac{1}{4}$ cups milk
1 (326-g/11$\frac{1}{2}$-oz/$\frac{3}{4}$-lb) can creamed sweetcorn
2–3 tomatoes, peeled, deseeded and chopped
salt and pepper
1 green or red pepper, deseeded and chopped

Melt the butter in a pan and fry the onion for 2–3 minutes without colouring. Stir in the flour, curry powder and tomato purée, then gradually add the stock and bring to the boil. Simmer for 10 minutes then add the milk, corn and tomatoes. Adjust the seasoning and simmer for 5 minutes.

Simmer the green or red pepper in boiling water for 5 minutes to soften. Drain and add to the soup.

Serves 4–6

Celery and ham soup

METRIC/IMPERIAL/AMERICAN
1 onion, chopped
1 head celery, trimmed and roughly chopped
50 g/2 oz/$\frac{1}{4}$ cup butter
600 ml/1 pint/2$\frac{1}{2}$ cups chicken stock
600 ml/1 pint/2$\frac{1}{2}$ cups milk
salt and pepper
bouquet garni
good pinch ground mace
25 g/1 oz/$\frac{1}{4}$ cup flour
75 g/3 oz/$\frac{1}{3}$ cup ham, chopped
paprika

Fry the onion and celery in the butter for 5–10 minutes without colouring. Add the stock, milk, seasoning, bouquet garni and mace, and bring to the boil. Cover and simmer for about 40 minutes until the celery is tender.

Remove the bouquet garni and then liquidise or sieve the soup. Return to the pan. Blend the flour with a little water, add a little of the soup, then whisk gradually into the rest of the soup. Add most of the ham, bring to the boil and simmer for 3–4 minutes. Adjust the seasoning and add the remaining ham. Serve lightly dusted with paprika.

Serves 6

Split pea soup

METRIC/IMPERIAL/AMERICAN
225 g/8 oz/1 cup split peas
1.75 litres/3 pints/7½ cups water
1 ham knuckle
1 onion, finely chopped
1 carrot, chopped
salt and pepper
1 bay leaf
½ teaspoon dried thyme

Soak the peas overnight in cold water. Drain and place in a pan with the measured water. Add the ham knuckle, onion, carrot, seasoning, bay leaf and thyme. Bring to the boil and skim if necessary. Cover and simmer for 2–2½ hours until the peas are tender. Remove the ham knuckle and bay leaf. Chop some of the ham and return to the soup. Adjust the seasoning and serve.
Note: This soup can be sieved or liquidised, if preferred.

Serves 6

Cream of pumpkin soup

METRIC/IMPERIAL/AMERICAN
1 onion, sliced
1.5 kg/3 lb/9 cups pumpkin, deseeded and chopped
50 g/2 oz/¼ cup butter
600 ml/1 pint/2½ cups chicken stock
600 ml/1 pint/2½ cups milk
salt and pepper
little ground nutmeg
4 tablespoons/4 tablespoons/⅓ cup cream
chopped parsley to garnish

Gently fry the onion and pumpkin in the melted butter for 5 minutes, until soft but not coloured. Add the stock and bring to the boil. Cover and simmer for about 1 hour until tender. Sieve or liquidise and return to the pan.

Add the milk and bring back to the boil, whisking continuously. Simmer for 5 minutes. Season well with salt, pepper and nutmeg, and stir in the cream. Reheat and serve sprinkled with the parsley.

Serves 6

Potato and bacon soup

METRIC/IMPERIAL/AMERICAN
175 g/6 oz/¾ cup streaky bacon rashers, derinded and
   finely chopped
1 large onion, finely chopped
350 g/12 oz/2 cups peeled potatoes, diced
generous litre/2 pints/5 cups chicken stock
2 bay leaves
salt and pepper
pinch ground mace
1 (198-g/7-oz/7-oz) can sweetcorn kernels, drained
1 tablespoon chopped parsley

Fry the bacon and onion in the fat from the bacon until
beginning to colour. Add the potatoes, stock, bay leaves,
seasoning and a pinch of mace. Bring to the boil, cover and
simmer for about 30 minutes until the potato has broken down.
Remove the bay leaves. Add the sweetcorn, adjust the
seasoning and simmer for a further 5 minutes. Stir in the parsley
and serve.

Serves 6

Creamed beetroot soup

METRIC/IMPERIAL/AMERICAN
50 g/2 oz/¼ cup butter
2 large onions, chopped
1 carrot, chopped
0.5 kg/1 lb/1 lb cooked beetroot, diced
1–2 tablespoons lemon juice
900 ml/1½ pints/3¾ cups beef stock
salt and pepper
300 ml/½ pint/1¼ cups milk
6 tablespoons/6 tablespoons/½ cup double cream

Melt the butter and fry the onion and carrot until beginning to
lightly brown. Add the beetroot, lemon juice, stock and
seasoning, and bring to the boil. Cover and simmer for 20–30
minutes then either sieve or liquidise the soup. Return the soup
to the pan with the milk and bring back to the boil. Adjust the
seasoning. Whip the cream lightly and add a spoonful to each
bowl of soup. Serve with pretzels.

Serves 6–8

Chicken and almond soup

METRIC/IMPERIAL/AMERICAN
chicken carcass plus trimmings
1.5 litres/2¾ pints/7 cups seasoned water
1 small onion, finely chopped
40 g/1½ oz/3 tablespoons butter
40 g/1½ oz/6 tablespoons flour
150 ml/¼ pint/⅔ cup milk or single cream
salt and pepper
pinch ground mace
50 g/2 oz/½ cup flaked almonds, toasted
1 tablespoon chopped parsley

Pick the meat off the carcass and chop finely to give
75–100 g/3–4 oz/½ cup. Boil the carcass in the seasoned water
for about 1 hour. Strain and use a generous litre/2 pints/5 cups
chicken stock.

Fry the onion in the butter until soft then stir in the flour and
cook for 1 minute. Gradually add the stock and bring to the
boil. Add the milk or cream, seasoning, mace and chopped
chicken, and simmer for 5–10 minutes. Just before serving,
adjust the seasoning, roughly chop most of the almonds and stir
into the soup with the parsley. Serve the remaining almonds
scattered over the top of the soup.

Serves 6

Smoked haddock soup

METRIC/IMPERIAL/AMERICAN
225 g/8 oz/½ lb smoked haddock (or 227-g/8-oz/8-oz
packet frozen smoked haddock)
1 onion, finely chopped
600 ml/1 pint/2½ cups water
600 ml/1 pint/2½ cups milk
salt and pepper
225–350 g/8–12 oz/1–1½ cups hot mashed potato
25 g/1 oz/2 tablespoons butter
lemon juice
chopped parsley

Place the fish in a pan with the onion and add the water. Bring
to the boil, cover and simmer gently until tender – about 15
minutes. Remove the fish, remove skin and bones and flake the
flesh finely. Return the skin and bones to the cooking liquor and
simmer for 10 minutes. Strain and return 450 ml/¾ pint/2 cups
liquor to the pan with the milk, flaked fish and seasoning. Bring
to the boil and simmer for 3 minutes, then gradually whisk in
sufficient mashed potato to give the required consistency. Stir in
the butter, sharpen to taste with lemon juice, adjust the
seasoning and serve sprinkled with parsley.
Note: This soup can be sieved or liquidised if a smoother soup
is preferred.

Serves 4–6

Stockpot soup

METRIC/IMPERIAL/AMERICAN
carcass of any cooked poultry or game
1.75 litres/3 pints/7½ cups water
salt and pepper
2 onions, finely chopped
2 carrots, chopped
1 leek, finely sliced and washed
1 parsnip, finely chopped
bouquet garni
good pinch ground mace
1 teaspoon tomato purée
good dash Worcestershire sauce
40 g/1½ oz/¼ cup long-grain rice
chopped parsley to garnish

Boil the carcass in the seasoned water for about 1 hour, to make a good stock. Strain and place a generous litre/2 pints/5 cups stock in a saucepan with any pieces of meat from the carcass and all the other ingredients, except the rice and parsley. Bring to the boil, cover and simmer for 30 minutes. Adjust the seasoning, add the rice and continue simmering for 15 minutes. Discard the bouquet garni and serve sprinkled with parsley.

Serves 4–6

Lentil soup with bacon

METRIC/IMPERIAL/AMERICAN
225 g/8 oz/1 cup lentils
1.5 litres/2½ pints/6¼ cups stock or water
1 onion, chopped
1 clove garlic, crushed
1 carrot, chopped
175 g/6 oz/¾ cup streaky bacon rashers, derinded and
    chopped
4 tomatoes, peeled and chopped
1 bay leaf
salt and pepper
225 g/8 oz/1⅓ cups potatoes, chopped
1 tablespoon wine vinegar
GARNISH:
chopped parsley
fried croûtons

Wash the lentils then soak them in the stock in a saucepan for 1–2 hours. Add the onion, garlic, carrot, bacon, tomatoes, bay leaf and seasoning. Bring to the boil, cover and simmer for about 1 hour or until the lentils are tender.

Add the potatoes and continue cooking for about 20 minutes or until tender. Remove the bay leaf, sieve or liquidise the soup and return to the pan. Adjust the seasoning, add the vinegar and reheat. Serve sprinkled with chopped parsley and fried croûtons.

Serves 6

Chilli beef chowder

METRIC/IMPERIAL/AMERICAN
25 g/1 oz/2 tablespoons butter
15 g/½ oz/1 tablespoon dripping
1 large onion, finely sliced
225 g/8 oz/1 cup raw beef, finely minced
2 tablespoons/2 tablespoons/3 tablespoons flour
1–2 teaspoons chilli powder
600 ml/1 pint/2½ cups beef stock
1–2 teaspoons tomato purée
3–4 tomatoes, peeled and chopped
1 (198-g/7-oz/7-oz) can red kidney beans, drained
salt and pepper

Melt the butter and dripping in a pan and fry the onion slowly
until soft. Stir in the minced beef and cook slowly for 10
minutes, stirring frequently. Add the flour and chilli powder
and cook for 1 minute. Gradually add the stock and tomato
purée, and bring to the boil. Cover and simmer for 25 minutes,
then stir in the tomatoes and beans. Season well and simmer for
a further 10 minutes. Adjust the seasoning and serve with crusty
French bread and butter.

Serves 4

Cream of pheasant soup

METRIC/IMPERIAL/AMERICAN
40 g/1½ oz/3 tablespoons butter
1 onion, very finely chopped
40 g/1½ oz/6 tablespoons flour
generous litre/2 pints/5 cups good pheasant stock
salt and pepper
ground mace
celery salt
25 g/1 oz/3 tablespoons long-grain rice (optional)
50–75 g/2–3 oz/⅓ cup cooked pheasant meat, chopped
4–6 tablespoons/4–6 tablespoons/⅓–½ cup single cream
GARNISH:
chopped parsley
fried croûtons

Melt the butter and fry the onion until softened. Stir in the flour
then gradually add the stock and bring to the boil. Season with
salt, pepper, mace and celery salt. Add the rice and simmer for
20 minutes, stirring occasionally. Sieve or liquidise if liked. Add
the pheasant and cream, and continue cooking gently for 3–4
minutes. Adjust the seasoning and garnish with parsley and
fried croûtons.

Serves 4–6

Cauliflower and mushroom soup

METRIC/IMPERIAL/AMERICAN
225 g/8 oz/2 cups mushrooms, chopped
1 onion, chopped
50 g/2 oz/$\frac{1}{4}$ cup butter
1 tablespoon flour
generous litre/2 pints/5 cups chicken stock
225 g/8 oz/$\frac{1}{2}$ lb raw cauliflower
salt and pepper
about 300 ml/$\frac{1}{2}$ pint/1$\frac{1}{4}$ cups milk
mint sprigs to garnish

Fry the mushrooms and onion gently in the butter until soft but not coloured. Add the flour and mix thoroughly. Gradually add the stock and bring to the boil, stirring. Cut the cauliflower into florets and add to the pan with plenty of seasoning. Cover and simmer for 25–30 minutes.

Sieve or liquidise the soup and return to the pan with sufficient milk to give the desired consistency. Adjust the seasoning, bring back to the boil for 2 minutes and serve garnished with mint sprigs.

Serves 6

Spinach soup

METRIC/IMPERIAL/AMERICAN
25 g/1 oz/2 tablespoons butter
1 onion, finely chopped
1 clove garlic, crushed
4 rashers lean bacon, derinded and finely chopped
1 (227-g/8-oz/$\frac{1}{2}$-lb) packet frozen chopped spinach
2 tablespoons/2 tablespoons/3 tablespoons flour
900 ml/1$\frac{1}{2}$ pints/3$\frac{3}{4}$ cups chicken stock
salt and pepper
ground nutmeg
25 g/1 oz/$\frac{1}{4}$ cup Cheddar cheese, finely grated

Melt the butter and fry the onion, garlic and bacon gently for 5 minutes. Add the spinach and cook gently until the spinach has thawed out, stirring frequently. Stir in the flour then whisk in the stock. Bring to the boil and season with salt, pepper and nutmeg. Cover and simmer for 25–30 minutes.

Either leave the soup as it is, or sieve or liquidise if a smooth soup is preferred. Return to the pan, bring back to the boil and adjust the seasoning. Serve sprinkled with cheese.

Serves 4–6

Cheese soup

METRIC/IMPERIAL/AMERICAN
40 g/1½ oz/3 tablespoons butter
2 onions, chopped
1 carrot, chopped
1 stick celery, chopped (optional)
25 g/1 oz/¼ cup flour
1 litre/1¾ pints/4¼ cups beef stock
salt and pepper
paprika
175 g/6 oz/1½ cups mature Cheddar cheese, finely grated
1 tablespoon chopped parsley

Melt the butter and fry the vegetables until soft and just beginning to colour. Stir in the flour, then gradually add the stock and bring to the boil. Season with salt, pepper and paprika. Cover and simmer for 20 minutes.

Sieve or liquidise the soup and return to the pan. Adjust the seasoning, bring back to the boil, then remove from the heat. Stir in 100 g/4 oz/1 cup of the cheese until melted, then add the parsley. Reheat gently and serve in bowls sprinkled with the remaining cheese.

Serves 4–6

Cream of cauliflower soup

METRIC/IMPERIAL/AMERICAN
1 large onion, chopped
50 g/2 oz/¼ cup butter
1 small cauliflower, trimmed and roughly chopped
600 ml/1 pint/2½ cups chicken stock
600 ml/1 pint/2½ cups milk
salt and pepper
1 bay leaf
2 blades mace
150 ml/¼ pint/⅔ cup cream
chopped parsley to garnish

Fry the onion in the butter until soft. Reserve a few florets of cauliflower for garnish. Add the remaining cauliflower to the onion and continue cooking gently for 5 minutes. Add the stock and milk and bring to the boil. Season, add the bay leaf and mace. Cover and simmer for 30–40 minutes until tender. Discard the bay leaf and mace.

Sieve or liquidise the soup and return to the pan. Adjust the seasoning and add the cream. Reheat without boiling and add the reserved florets of cauliflower. Sprinkle with parsley and serve with Melba toast.

Serves 6

Bortsch

METRIC/IMPERIAL/AMERICAN
0.5 kg/1 lb/1 lb raw beetroot, grated
2 carrots, chopped
1 onion, chopped
1 bay leaf
generous litre/2 pints/5 cups chicken stock
salt and pepper
lemon juice
150 ml/¼ pint/⅔ cup soured cream

Put the beetroot into a saucepan with the carrots, onion, bay leaf, stock and seasoning. Bring to the boil, cover and simmer for about 45 minutes. Strain the soup and return to the pan. Adjust the seasoning and sharpen with lemon juice. Bring back to the boil and serve each portion with a spoonful of soured cream.

Note: This soup can also be served chilled with the cream addition as above.

Serves 6

Oxtail soup

METRIC/IMPERIAL/AMERICAN
1 oxtail, jointed
15 g/½ oz/1 tablespoon dripping
2 onions, finely chopped
1 carrot, finely chopped
2 sticks celery, finely chopped
½ leek, finely chopped
2 litres/3½ pints/9 cups beef stock
bouquet garni
salt and pepper
25 g/1 oz/¼ cup flour
1 tablespoon lemon juice
sherry (optional)
chopped parsley to garnish

Wash and dry the oxtail, removing any fat. Fry in the dripping with all the vegetables for about 10 minutes or until evenly browned. Add the stock, bouquet garni and seasoning, and bring to the boil. Cover and simmer for 3–4 hours until the meat is tender. Skim the fat from the pan occasionally.

Remove the meat from the pan and discard the bouquet garni. Sieve or liquidise the soup and return to the pan. Blend the flour with the lemon juice and a little water and whisk into the soup. Bring to the boil and adjust the seasoning. Chop the meat from the bones and return to the pan. Add sherry to taste and simmer for 3–4 minutes. Garnish with the parsley.

Serves 6–8

Pepper and tomato soup

METRIC/IMPERIAL/AMERICAN
1 large onion, chopped
2 rashers bacon, chopped
1 clove garlic, crushed
2 tablespoons/2 tablespoons/3 tablespoons dripping
2 red peppers, deseeded and chopped
350 g/12 oz/2 cups tomatoes, peeled and chopped
generous litre/2 pints/5 cups beef stock
1 bay leaf
salt and pepper
1 tablespoon wine vinegar
6 tablespoons/6 tablespoons/$\frac{1}{2}$ cup single cream
  (optional)

Fry the onion, bacon and garlic gently in the dripping for 5 minutes. Add most of the pepper and all of the tomatoes and cook gently for 10 minutes. Add the stock, bay leaf, seasoning and vinegar. Bring to the boil, cover and simmer for 40 minutes.

Remove the bay leaf then sieve or liquidise the soup. Return to the pan, adjust the seasoning. Blanch the remaining pepper in boiling water for 5 minutes. Drain and stir into the soup. Serve with a tablespoon of cream swirled into each serving, if liked.

Serves 6

Thick vegetable soup

METRIC/IMPERIAL/AMERICAN
100 g/4 oz/4 oz each carrot, onion, celery, turnip and
  parsnip, chopped
1 leek, trimmed, sliced and washed
50 g/2 oz/$\frac{1}{4}$ cup butter
25 g/1 oz/$\frac{1}{4}$ cup flour
2 large tomatoes, peeled and sliced
1 teaspoon tomato purée
1 litre/1$\frac{3}{4}$ pints/4$\frac{1}{4}$ cups beef stock
2 bay leaves
good pinch ground nutmeg
salt and pepper
300 ml/$\frac{1}{2}$ pint/1$\frac{1}{4}$ cups milk
rings of leek to garnish

Gently fry the vegetables (except the tomatoes) in the melted butter for about 10 minutes without colouring. Stir in the flour and cook for 1 minute. Add the tomatoes, tomato purée, stock, bay leaves, nutmeg and seasoning. Bring to the boil, cover and simmer gently for 30 minutes. Remove the bay leaves, sieve or liquidise the soup and return to the pan with the milk. Bring back to the boil and simmer for a few minutes. Adjust the seasoning and serve garnished with rings of leek.

Serves 6

Chilled soups

Cold soups are ideal to serve on a warm summer's day. As soups freeze so well, they can be made in advance to save time when preparing a lunch or dinner party. When freezing soups, do not add cream or egg yolks until the soup is thawed. Refreshing chilled soups make good picnic fare and can be transported in a vacuum flask.

Cucumber soup

METRIC/IMPERIAL/AMERICAN
1 large cucumber, diced
900 ml/1½ pints/3¾ cups chicken stock
2 tablespoons/2 tablespoons/3 tablespoons finely chopped onion
25 g/1 oz/2 tablespoons butter
20 g/¾ oz/3 tablespoons flour
salt and pepper
little lemon juice
green food colouring (optional)
2 egg yolks
4 tablespoons/4 tablespoons/⅓ cup single cream
GARNISH:
mint sprigs
cucumber slices

Place the cucumber in a saucepan with the stock and onion. Bring to the boil, cover and simmer for about 20 minutes until the cucumber is tender. Cool then sieve or liquidise.

Melt the butter in a pan, stir in the flour and cook for 1 minute, then gradually add the cucumber purée. Bring to the boil, stirring frequently, simmer for 2 minutes then season to taste with salt, pepper and lemon juice. Add a little green food colouring, if liked. Blend the egg yolks into the cream then whisk in a little of the soup. Return this mixture to the pan and reheat gently, whisking continuously, to just below boiling point. Cool then chill thoroughly. Serve garnished with mint sprigs on cucumber slices.

Serves 6

Gazpacho

METRIC/IMPERIAL/AMERICAN
600 ml/1 pint/2½ cups canned tomato juice, well chilled
2 teaspoons wine vinegar
2 tablespoons/2 tablespoons/3 tablespoons lemon juice
½ teaspoon Worcestershire sauce
2 cloves garlic, crushed
salt and freshly ground black pepper
225 g/8 oz/1⅓ cups tomatoes, peeled and chopped
½ small onion, peeled and grated
1 (5-cm/2-inch/2-inch) piece cucumber, coarsely grated
½ green pepper, deseeded and finely chopped
ice cubes
chopped parsley to garnish

Place the tomato juice in a bowl with the vinegar, lemon juice, Worcestershire sauce, garlic and seasoning to taste. Add the tomatoes, onion, cucumber and pepper, and mix well. Sieve or liquidise, if liked. Cover the bowl and chill thoroughly.

Place in bowls with 2–3 ice cubes in each and garnish with parsley. Serve this soup with a dish of chopped cucumber, green pepper and tomato wedges.

Serves 4

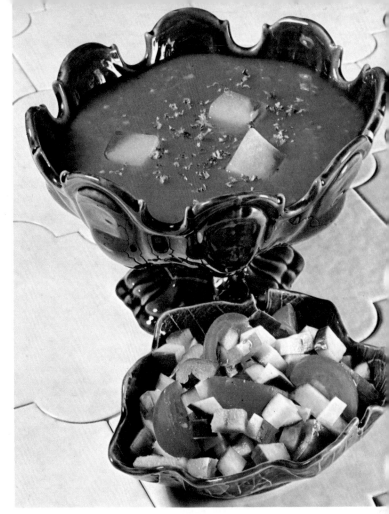

Vichysoisse

METRIC/IMPERIAL/AMERICAN
3 leeks
40 g/1½ oz/3 tablespoons butter
1 onion, thinly sliced
0.5 kg/1 lb/1 lb potatoes, peeled and chopped
900 ml/1½ pints/3¾ cups chicken or veal stock
salt and pepper
pinch ground nutmeg
1 egg yolk
150 ml/¼ pint/⅔ cup single cream
snipped chives to garnish

Clean the leeks, removing most of the green part. Finely slice the remainder. Melt the butter in a pan and sauté the leeks and onion for 5 minutes without browning. Add the potatoes, stock, seasoning and nutmeg, and bring to the boil. Cover and simmer for about 30 minutes or until all the vegetables are soft.

Sieve or liquidise the soup and return to the pan. Blend the egg yolk into the cream, whisk into the soup and reheat gently without boiling. Adjust the seasoning, cool and chill thoroughly. Serve sprinkled with the chives.

Serves 4–6

Cream of curry soup

METRIC/IMPERIAL/AMERICAN
2 large onions, chopped
1 clove garlic, crushed
40 g/1½ oz/3 tablespoons butter or margarine
2 teaspoons curry powder
2 tablespoons/2 tablespoons/3 tablespoons flour
900 ml/1½ pints/3¾ cups chicken stock
juice of ½ lemon
salt and pepper
good dash Tabasco sauce
pinch paprika
1 bay leaf
150 ml/¼ pint/⅔ cup milk
150 ml/¼ pint/⅔ cup single cream
1 large carrot, grated

Fry the onion and garlic in the butter until soft but not coloured. Stir in the curry powder and flour, then gradually add the stock and bring to the boil. Add the lemon juice, salt, pepper, Tabasco sauce, paprika and bay leaf. Cover and simmer gently for about 20 minutes or until the onion is tender.

Remove the bay leaf and sieve or liquidise the soup. Return to the pan and adjust the seasoning. Cool then stir in the milk and cream. Chill very thoroughly. Just before serving, stir in the grated carrot. Serve with hot garlic bread, if liked.
Note: More curry powder may be added.

Serves 6

Cream of artichoke soup

METRIC/IMPERIAL/AMERICAN
1 large onion, chopped
50 g/2 oz/¼ cup butter
0.75 kg/1½ lb/1½ lb Jerusalem artichokes
generous litre/2 pints/5 cups chicken stock
salt and pepper
1 bay leaf
1 blade mace
1 tablespoon lemon juice
150 ml/¼ pint/⅔ cup single cream
chopped parsley or fried croûtons to garnish

Gently fry the onion in the butter until soft but not coloured. Peel and slice the artichokes, add to the pan and toss in the butter for a few minutes. Add the stock, seasoning, bay leaf, mace and lemon juice. Bring to the boil, cover and simmer for about 30 minutes or until tender. Discard the bay leaf and mace.

Sieve or liquidise the soup, adjust the seasoning, cool and chill. Just before serving, stir in the cream and garnish with parsley or croûtons.
Note: This soup can also be served hot.

Serves 6

Cream of asparagus soup

METRIC/IMPERIAL/AMERICAN

0.5 kg/1 lb/1 lb fresh asparagus
1 small onion, chopped
salt and pepper
600 ml/1 pint/2½ cups chicken stock
40 g/1½ oz/3 tablespoons butter
25 g/1 oz/¼ cup flour
300 ml/½ pint/1¼ cups milk
150 ml/¼ pint/⅔ cup cream

Wash and trim the asparagus, removing all the hard woody stem. Cut the remainder into short lengths, keeping a few tips aside for garnish. Cook these tips in salted water for a few minutes until tender, then drain. Place the remaining asparagus, onion and seasoning in a pan with the stock. Cover and simmer for about 20 minutes until tender. Sieve or liquidise.

Melt the butter in a pan, stir in the flour and cook for 1 minute. Gradually add the milk and bring to the boil, stirring; then add the asparagus purée. Simmer gently for 5 minutes and adjust the seasoning. Cool, stir in the cream and chill. Serve garnished with the reserved cooked asparagus tips.
Note: This soup can also be served hot.

Serves 6

Cream of watercress soup

METRIC/IMPERIAL/AMERICAN

1 small onion, chopped
50 g/2 oz/¼ cup butter
2 bunches watercress, stalks removed
225 g/8 oz/1¼ cups potatoes, cooked and diced
900 ml/1½ pints/3¾ cups milk
salt and pepper
150 ml/¼ pint/⅔ cup single cream
watercress sprigs to garnish

Sauté the onion in the butter until soft then add the roughly chopped watercress and continue cooking for a few minutes. Stir in the potatoes and milk. Season well and bring to the boil. Simmer for 5 minutes, adjust the seasoning and cool slightly. Sieve or liquidise the soup. Stir in the cream and chill. Garnish each bowl of soup with a sprig of watercress.

Serves 6

Chilled avocado soup

METRIC/IMPERIAL/AMERICAN
2 tablespoons/2 tablespoons/3 tablespoons finely chopped
  onion
40 g/1½ oz/3 tablespoons butter
25 g/1 oz/¼ cup flour
750 ml/1¼ pints/3 cups chicken stock
2 medium ripe avocados
1–2 teaspoons lemon juice
salt and pepper
150 ml/¼ pint/⅔ cup milk
150 ml/¼ pint/⅔ cup cream
slices of avocado to garnish

Fry the onion gently in the butter for 3–5 minutes without
colouring. Add the flour and cook for 1 minute. Gradually add
the stock and bring to the boil. Simmer for 5 minutes. Quarter
the avocados, remove the stones and peel. (Reserve a few slices
to garnish.) Roughly chop the avocado flesh and add to the
soup with the lemon juice and seasoning. Simmer for 3–4
minutes.

Sieve or liquidise, stir in the milk and cream, and adjust the
seasoning. Cool then chill thoroughly. Serve garnished with the
slices of avocado.

Serves 4

Curried prawn soup

METRIC/IMPERIAL/AMERICAN
50 g/2 oz/¼ cup butter
1 onion, chopped
2 carrots, chopped
2 sticks celery, chopped
1–1½ teaspoons curry powder
2 tablespoons/2 tablespoons/3 tablespoons flour
600 ml/1 pint/2½ cups fish stock (or chicken stock)
175 g/6 oz/1 cup peeled prawns
salt and pepper
dash Tabasco sauce
1 tablespoon lemon juice
about 450 ml/¾ pint/2 cups creamy milk
GARNISH:
chopped parsley
whole unshelled prawns

Melt the butter and fry the vegetables until soft and just
beginning to colour. Stir in the curry powder and flour, then
add the stock and bring to the boil. Add 100 g/4 oz/⅔ cup
prawns, seasoning, Tabasco sauce and lemon juice. Cover and
simmer for 30 minutes.

Sieve or liquidise the soup and return to the pan with
sufficient milk to give the required consistency. Adjust the
seasoning. Roughly chop the remaining prawns and add to the
soup. Cool, then chill thoroughly. Serve garnished with the
parsley and whole unshelled prawns.

Serves 4–6

Cream of spinach soup

METRIC/IMPERIAL/AMERICAN
0.5 kg/1 lb/1 lb spinach
50 g/2 oz/¼ cup butter
1 onion, chopped
900 ml/1½ pints/3¾ cups chicken stock
salt and pepper
good pinch ground nutmeg
2–3 teaspoons lemon juice
1 bay leaf
6 tablespoons/6 tablespoons/½ cup double cream
fried croûtons to garnish

Wash the spinach thoroughly, discarding any tough stalks. Roughly chop the spinach. Melt the butter in a pan and fry the onion gently until soft but not coloured. Add the spinach and sauté gently for 5 minutes, stirring frequently. Add the stock, seasoning, nutmeg, lemon juice and bay leaf. Bring to the boil, cover and simmer for about 20 minutes.

Discard the bay leaf then sieve or liquidise the soup. Return to the pan, bring back to the boil for 2 minutes and adjust the seasoning. Cool then chill thoroughly. Stir in the cream just before serving in soup bowls with fried bread croûtons.
Note: This soup can also be served hot.

Serves 4–6

Fennel soup

METRIC/IMPERIAL/AMERICAN
1 bulb fennel, chopped
1 onion, chopped
900 ml/1½ pints/3¾ cups chicken stock
25 g/1 oz/2 tablespoons butter
25 g/1 oz/¼ cup flour
salt and pepper
juice of ½ lemon
1 tablespoon chopped parsley
4 tablespoons/4 tablespoons/⅓ cup cream
fennel sprigs to garnish

Place the fennel and onion in a saucepan with the stock and bring to the boil. Cover and simmer for 20–30 minutes until tender. Sieve or liquidise.

Melt the butter in a pan, stir in the flour and cook for 1 minute. Gradually add the fennel purée and bring to the boil. Season well, add the lemon juice and chopped parsley. Simmer for 3–4 minutes, stirring. Cool then stir in the cream and chill thoroughly. Garnish with the feathery top part of the fennel.

Serves 4–6

Apricot and apple soup

METRIC/IMPERIAL/AMERICAN
100 g/4 oz/¾ cup dried apricots, soaked overnight
0.5 kg/1 lb/1 lb eating apples
1 tablespoon lemon juice
750 ml/1¼ pints/3 cups chicken stock
6 tablespoons/6 tablespoons/½ cup dry white wine
pinch ground ginger
salt and pepper
GARNISH:
4 tablespoons/4 tablespoons/⅓ cup soured cream
ground ginger

Drain the apricots and place in a saucepan with the peeled, cored and chopped apples, lemon juice and stock. Bring to the boil, cover and simmer gently until all the fruit is soft and broken down.

Sieve or liquidise then return to the pan. Add the wine, ginger and a little seasoning. Cool then chill thoroughly. Serve with a spoonful of soured cream on each portion, topped with a dusting of ground ginger.

Serves 4

Hollandaise soup

METRIC/IMPERIAL/AMERICAN
2 carrots, finely diced
1 onion, finely diced
40 g/1½ oz/3 tablespoons butter or oil
25 g/1 oz/¼ cup flour
900 ml/1½ pints/3¾ cups chicken stock
salt and pepper
2 egg yolks
150 ml/¼ pint/⅔ cup single cream
2 teaspoons wine vinegar
freshly chopped mint, chives and parsley to garnish

Fry the carrot and onion gently in the butter or oil until soft, then stir in the flour. Cook for 1 minute then gradually add the stock and bring to the boil. Season well, cover and simmer for about 30 minutes until the vegetables are tender. Sieve or liquidise, if liked.

Whisk the egg yolks into the cream, add a little of the soup then whisk it all back into the remainder of the soup. Add the vinegar, bring just up to the boil and adjust the seasoning. Cool, chill and serve sprinkled with the mixed fresh herbs.
Note: This soup is also very good served hot.

Serves 4

Iced lemon soup

METRIC/IMPERIAL/AMERICAN
1 onion, chopped
1 clove garlic, crushed (optional)
40 g/1½ oz/3 tablespoons butter
25 g/1 oz/¼ cup flour
900 ml/1½ pints/3¾ cups good chicken stock
grated rind and juice of 1 large lemon
salt and pepper
1 bay leaf
300 ml/½ pint/1¼ cups single cream
GARNISH:
thin slices of lemon
mint sprigs

Fry the onion and garlic in the butter until soft but not coloured. Stir in the flour then gradually add the stock and bring to the boil. Add the lemon rind and juice, seasoning and bay leaf. Cover and simmer for 20 minutes.

Remove the bay leaf, sieve or liquidise the soup and place in a bowl. Stir in the cream and adjust the seasoning. Cool then chill thoroughly. Garnish with thin slices of lemon floating on each portion and a sprig of mint. Serve with breadsticks.

Serves 6

Jellied consommé

METRIC/IMPERIAL/AMERICAN
1 recipe hot consommé (see page 11)
2–3 teaspoons powdered gelatine (see method)
1 tablespoon chopped mixed herbs
julienne strips of orange rind to garnish

If you use a good enough stock which jellies by itself you will not need to add gelatine, but if you use stock cubes or a weak stock then dissolve the gelatine in 3 tablespoons/3 tablespoons/¼ cup consommé in a bowl over a pan of hot water. Add this to the consommé. Stir in the mixed herbs, then chill until set. Serve roughly chopped in soup bowls and garnish with the orange rind, which has been boiled until tender. Serve with Melba toast.

Serves 6

Pâtés

A pâté makes an impressive start to a meal. It can be smooth or coarse textured and is usually served with thin slices of toast or crackers. The recipes in this chapter include ones for both meat and fish pâtés. Pâtés may also be served as a main course with an accompanying salad.

Rosie's pâté

METRIC/IMPERIAL/AMERICAN
2 large onions, chopped
2–3 cloves garlic, crushed
225 g/8 oz/1 cup streaky bacon, derinded and chopped
2 tablespoons/2 tablespoons/3 tablespoons oil
225 g/8 oz/1 cup belly pork, derinded and chopped
0.5 kg/1 lb/1 lb pig's liver, roughly chopped
150 ml/¼ pint/⅔ cup red wine
150 ml/¼ pint/⅔ cup beef stock
2 bay leaves
salt and black pepper
1 teaspoon Worcestershire sauce
GARNISH:
mustard and cress
slices of cucumber
lemon butterflies

Fry the onion, garlic and bacon in the oil until soft. Add the pork and liver and continue cooking for 5–10 minutes. Add all other ingredients. Bring to the boil, cover and simmer for about 40 minutes.

Remove the bay leaves, cool slightly then mince finely. Adjust the seasoning. Pack into a greased 1-kg/2-lb/2-lb loaf tin and stand in a roasting tin containing a 2.5-cm/1-inch depth of water. Cook in a moderately hot oven (180°C, 350°F, Gas Mark 4) for 1 hour. Cool, place a weight on top and chill before turning out. Garnish and serve with toast.

Serves 10

34

Chicken liver pâté

METRIC/IMPERIAL/AMERICAN
1 onion, very finely chopped
1–2 cloves garlic, crushed
50 g/2 oz/$\frac{1}{4}$ cup butter
0.5 kg/1 lb/1 lb chicken livers
salt and black pepper
2 tablespoons/2 tablespoons/3 tablespoons double cream
2 tablespoons/2 tablespoons/3 tablespoons red wine
melted butter
GARNISH:
capers
bay leaves

Fry the onion and garlic in the butter until soft but not coloured. Wash and drain the chicken livers thoroughly, add to the pan and cook gently for 10 minutes, stirring occasionally to prevent sticking. Remove from the heat and beat in the seasoning, cream and wine.

Sieve or liquidise the pâté, adjust the seasoning and pack into 6 individual dishes. Cover the tops with melted butter and chill thoroughly. Garnish with capers and a bay leaf. The garnish may be put on before pouring over the melted butter.

Serves 6

Farmhouse pâté

METRIC/IMPERIAL/AMERICAN
175 g/6 oz/6 oz pig's liver
175 g/6 oz/6 oz stewing steak
175 g/6 oz/6 oz lean belly pork
1 large onion
1–2 cloves garlic, crushed
25 g/1 oz/$\frac{1}{2}$ cup fresh breadcrumbs
1 large egg, beaten
salt and pepper
good pinch ground nutmeg
3–4 tablespoons/3–4 tablespoons/$\frac{1}{4}$–$\frac{1}{3}$ cup red or white wine
175 g/6 oz/6 oz streaky bacon rashers, derinded
GARNISH:
chopped red pepper
chopped cucumber

Coarsely mince the liver, steak, pork and onion. Add the garlic, breadcrumbs, egg, seasoning, nutmeg and wine, and mix very thoroughly. Line a 0.5-kg/1-lb/1-lb loaf tin with the streaky bacon (stretched with the back of a knife) and spoon in the pâté mixture. Press down evenly and fold over the ends of the bacon. Stand the pâté in a roasting tin containing a 2.5-cm/1-inch depth of water. Cook in a moderately hot oven (180°C, 350°F, Gas Mark 4) for 1$\frac{1}{2}$–2 hours. Cool with a weight on top. Serve in slices garnished with chopped red pepper and cucumber, and with hot toast and butter.

Serves 6–8

Liver and bacon pâté

METRIC/IMPERIAL/AMERICAN
0.75 kg/1½ lb/1½ lb pig's liver
1 onion
2 cloves garlic, crushed
350 g/12 oz/¾ lb streaky bacon rashers, derinded
25 g/1 oz/½ cup fresh breadcrumbs
salt and pepper
2 tablespoons/2 tablespoons/3 tablespoons brandy or red wine
1 egg, beaten
3 bay leaves
slices of celery to garnish

Put half the liver in a saucepan, cover with water and simmer for 5 minutes. Drain. Mince together finely with the remaining raw liver, onion, garlic and half the bacon. Mix in the breadcrumbs, seasoning, brandy and egg.

Lay the bay leaves in the base of a 0.5-kg/1-lb/1-lb loaf tin. Stretch the remaining rashers with the back of a knife and use to line the inside of the tin. Fill with the liver mixture and fold over the ends of the bacon. Stand the pâté in a roasting tin containing a 2.5-cm/1-inch depth of water. Cook in a moderately hot oven (180°C, 350°F, Gas Mark 4) for 1½–2 hours. Cool, cover with a weighted plate and chill before turning out. Garnish with the celery slices and serve with Melba or hot buttered toast.

Serves 10

Sardine pâté

METRIC/IMPERIAL/AMERICAN
2 (120-g/4¼-oz/4¼-oz) cans sardines in oil, drained
75 g/3 oz/6 tablespoons cream cheese (Philadelphia)
½ teaspoon grated lemon rind
1 tablespoon very finely chopped onion
1 hard-boiled egg, mashed
1–2 tablespoons/1–2 tablespoons/1–3 tablespoons lemon juice
2 tablespoons/2 tablespoons/3 tablespoons cream or natural yogurt
salt and black pepper
garlic powder
GARNISH:
slices of tomato
chopped green pepper
parsley sprigs

Mash the sardines thoroughly. Soften the cream cheese and beat into the sardines with the lemon rind, onion and mashed egg. Add the lemon juice and cream, and mix to give a smooth consistency. Season to taste with salt, pepper and garlic powder. Either serve in individual ramekin dishes or a larger dish garnished with tomato slices, chopped green pepper and parsley sprigs. Hand fingers of hot brown toast separately.

Serves 4–6

Smoked mackerel pâté

METRIC/IMPERIAL/AMERICAN
225 g/8 oz/½ lb smoked mackerel
50 g/2 oz/1 cup fresh white breadcrumbs
grated rind of ½ lemon
2 tablespoons/2 tablespoons/3 tablespoons lemon juice
salt and pepper
little garlic powder
2 teaspoons finely chopped onion
50 g/2 oz/¼ cup butter, melted
4–6 tablespoons/4–6 tablespoons/⅓–½ cup cream
GARNISH:
slices of tomato
slices of cucumber
parsley sprigs

Remove the skin and bones from the fish and mash thoroughly.
Add the breadcrumbs, lemon rind and juice, seasoning, garlic
powder, onion and melted butter, mix very thoroughly. Add
sufficient cream to give a softish consistency and divide between
4–6 ramekin dishes or plates. Chill thoroughly and garnish with
the tomato and cucumber slices, parsley sprigs and serve with
toast.

Serves 4–6

Kipper pâté

METRIC/IMPERIAL/AMERICAN
5–8 frozen kipper fillets
2 tablespoons/2 tablespoons/3 tablespoons finely chopped
    onion
50 g/2 oz/¼ cup butter
½ teaspoon finely grated lemon rind
about 2 teaspoons lemon juice
salt and pepper
little garlic powder (optional)
2 tablespoons/2 tablespoons/3 tablespoons cream
GARNISH:
lettuce leaves
watercress
slices of lemon
tomato wedges

Cook the kippers according to the instructions on the packet.
Cool, remove the skin and bones, and flake the flesh. Fry the
onion in the butter until soft then beat into the kippers with the
lemon rind and juice. Season with a little salt, plenty of pepper
and a pinch of garlic powder, if liked. Beat in the cream until the
pâté is smooth. Sharpen with more lemon juice, if necessary.
Pile on to individual dishes or one large dish and chill. Garnish
with the lettuce, watercress, lemon slices and tomato. Serve
with plenty of hot toast and butter, or Melba toast.

Serves 6

Salads

Salads make interesting starters with their attractive colours, varying textures and flavours. When purchasing salad vegetables reject ones that are not fresh and crisp, as stale vegetables will not do justice to any finished dish. If adding a dressing either serve separately or pour it over just before serving, to retain the crispness of the dish.

Salad niçoise

METRIC/IMPERIAL/AMERICAN
lettuce leaves
1 (198-g/7-oz/7-oz) can tuna, drained and flaked
1 green pepper, deseeded and sliced
1 tablespoon finely chopped onion
3 large tomatoes, each cut into six
175 g/6 oz/6 oz French beans, cooked
1 tablespoon capers
6 tablespoons/6 tablespoons/$\frac{1}{2}$ cup French dressing
GARNISH:
3 hard-boiled eggs
$\frac{1}{2}$ (50-g/$1\frac{3}{4}$-oz/$1\frac{3}{4}$-oz) can anchovy fillets, drained
black olives

Arrange the lettuce leaves on 6 small plates or dishes. Lightly toss together the tuna, green pepper, onion, tomatoes, beans, capers and dressing. Spoon over the lettuce leaves. Garnish with quarters of hard-boiled egg, anchovy fillets and black olives. Serve with French bread.

Serves 6

Tuna bean salad

METRIC/IMPERIAL/AMERICAN
2 green eating apples, cored and chopped
1 tablespoon lemon juice
1 (198-g/7-oz/7-oz) can tuna, flaked
1 tablespoon finely chopped onion
3 sticks celery, sliced
1 (425-g/15-oz/15-oz) can red kidney beans, drained
salt and pepper
4–5 tablespoons/4–5 tablespoons/5–6 tablespoons French dressing
watercress to garnish

Dip the apple in the lemon juice, then place in a bowl with the tuna, onion, celery and red kidney beans. Season well, add the dressing and toss thoroughly. Leave to stand for about 30 minutes before serving on small plates. Garnish with watercress and serve with French bread and butter.

Serves 4–6

Victorian cocktail

METRIC/IMPERIAL/AMERICAN
3 grapefruit
2 ripe avocados
4 tablespoons/4 tablespoons/⅓ cup French dressing
mint sprigs to garnish

Using a sharp knife, cut the top and bottom off each grapefruit. Stand the grapefruit on one end and cut away all the peel and pith together in a downward movement. Cut between the membranes and ease out the segments. Place the segments in a bowl with any juice.

Cut the avocados into quarters lengthways, then remove the stones and peel carefully. Cut the flesh into cubes and add to the grapefruit. Toss thoroughly in the grapefruit juice. Chill. Spoon into 4 individual dishes with a little grapefruit juice in each. Add 1 tablespoon French dressing to each dish, garnish with a mint sprig and serve.

Serves 4

Hidden peaches

METRIC/IMPERIAL/AMERICAN
1 (425-g/15-oz/16-oz) can white peach halves
40 g/1½ oz/½ cup blue cheese, crumbled
15 g/½ oz/1 tablespoon butter, softened
150 ml/¼ pint/⅔ cup single cream
salt and pepper
paprika
1 small lettuce
75 g/3 oz/6 tablespoons soft cream cheese

Drain 4 peach halves. Mash the blue cheese and mix with the butter, 1 tablespoon of the cream, seasoning and paprika to taste. Use to fill the stone cavities of the peaches.
   Arrange the lettuce on 4 small plates and place a peach on each with the rounded side upwards. Soften the cream cheese then beat in sufficient cream to give a coating consistency. Spoon carefully over the peaches until completely masked. Sprinkle with paprika and serve with triangles of toast.

Serves 4

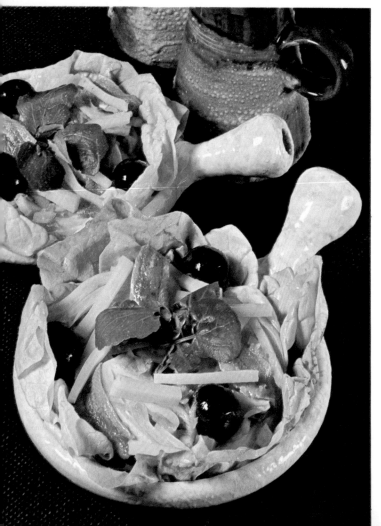

Fennel salad

METRIC/IMPERIAL/AMERICAN
1 bulb Florence fennel, chopped
1 tablespoon finely chopped onion
2 carrots, coarsely grated
1 (50-g/1¾-oz/1¾-oz) can anchovy fillets, drained
few black olives, stoned
6 tablespoons/6 tablespoons/½ cup French dressing
salt and pepper
1 small lettuce
50 g/2 oz/2 oz Emmenthal cheese, cut into julienne strips

Place the fennel in a bowl with the onion and grated carrot. Cut the anchovy fillets into 2.5-cm/1-inch lengths and add to the salad with a few black olives. Add the dressing and seasoning, and leave to stand for about 20 minutes. Arrange lettuce leaves in 4 small dishes and spoon the salad on top. Place cheese strips over the salad and top each with an olive.

Serves 4

Dressed French beans

METRIC/IMPERIAL/AMERICAN
0.5 kg/1 lb/1 lb French beans, trimmed
salt and pepper
150 ml/¼ pint/⅔ cup French dressing
1 clove garlic, crushed
GARNISH:
4 tomatoes, sliced
2 hard-boiled eggs, chopped

Cook the beans in boiling salted water until just tender – do not overcook. Drain well and place in a bowl. Add the dressing, garlic and seasoning to the hot beans and mix lightly. Cool then chill.

Arrange the beans on small plates, garnish with the sliced tomatoes round the edge and sprinkle with the chopped hard-boiled egg. Serve with brown bread and butter, if liked.

Serves 4

Minted tomato salad

METRIC/IMPERIAL/AMERICAN
0.5 kg/1 lb/1 lb tomatoes
salt and pepper
freshly chopped mint
6 tablespoons/6 tablespoons/½ cup soured cream
good pinch sugar
¼ teaspoon grated lemon rind
1 tablespoon lemon juice
crisp lettuce leaves
mint sprigs to garnish

Peel the tomatoes, quarter and remove the pips. Sprinkle lightly with salt and pepper and 1 teaspoon chopped mint. Season the cream, adding the pinch of sugar, lemon rind and juice and 1 tablespoon chopped mint.

Arrange crisp lettuce in 4 small dishes, lay the tomatoes on top and spoon the creamy dressing over them. Garnish with the sprigs of mint and serve with Melba or French toast.

Serves 4

Chicory and apple cocktail

METRIC/IMPERIAL/AMERICAN
2 red-skinned apples
1 green-skinned apple
1 tablespoon lemon juice
3 tablespoons/3 tablespoons/$\frac{1}{4}$ cup French dressing
salt and pepper
2 heads chicory, sliced
2 carrots, coarsely grated
watercress sprigs to garnish

Quarter, core and chop 1 red and the green apple. Dip in the lemon juice then add the dressing and seasoning. Add the chicory and grated carrots, and toss thoroughly. Arrange on 4 small plates. Slice the remaining apple and use to garnish the starter together with the watercress.

Serves 4

Artichokes niçoise

METRIC/IMPERIAL/AMERICAN
1 (425-g/15-oz/16-oz) can artichoke hearts, drained
2 tablespoons/2 tablespoons/3 tablespoons chopped onion
150 ml/$\frac{1}{4}$ pint/$\frac{2}{3}$ cup French dressing
salt and black pepper
1 (50-g/1$\frac{3}{4}$-oz/1$\frac{3}{4}$-oz) can anchovy fillets, drained
12 black olives
watercress to garnish

Cut the artichoke hearts into halves or quarters, depending on size, and place in a bowl with the onion, dressing and seasoning. Cut the anchovies into 2.5-cm/1-inch lengths and add to the bowl with the olives. Toss lightly and leave to stand for about 20 minutes. Arrange the salad in 4 small dishes and garnish with watercress.

Serves 4

Vegetable and fruit starters

These, like salads, are seasonal starters. Make sure the vegetables and fruits are fresh and sound. Some vegetables and fruit may be combined in a dish to make an interesting and unusual starter – see the recipe on page 45 for leek and pineapple cocktails.

Stuffed aubergines

METRIC/IMPERIAL/AMERICAN
1 onion, finely chopped
2 lean rashers bacon, derinded and chopped
25 g/1 oz/2 tablespoons butter
2 medium aubergines
175 g/6 oz/1 cup tomatoes, peeled and chopped
1 teaspoon tomato purée
salt and pepper
good pinch garlic powder
75 g/3 oz/¾ cup Emmenthal cheese, grated
parsley sprigs to garnish

Fry the onion and bacon in the butter until just beginning to colour. Cut the aubergines in half lengthways and scoop out the flesh, leaving a thin layer inside the skin. Chop the flesh and add to the pan with the tomatoes, tomato purée, seasoning and garlic powder. Cook gently for about 5 minutes. Remove from the heat and stir in 50 g/2 oz/½ cup of the cheese. Spoon into the aubergine shells, place in an ovenproof dish and sprinkle with the remaining cheese. Bake in a moderately hot oven (200°C, 400°F, Gas Mark 6) for 30–40 minutes until the aubergine is tender and the cheese brown and bubbling. Serve hot, garnished with the parsley.

Serves 4

Mushrooms in garlic butter

METRIC/IMPERIAL/AMERICAN
75 g/3 oz/6 tablespoons butter
1 tablespoon oil
2–3 large cloves garlic, crushed
2 tablespoons/2 tablespoons/3 tablespoons grated onion
350–450 g/¾–1 lb/3–4 cups button mushrooms, trimmed
salt and freshly ground black pepper
GARNISH:
1 tablespoon freshly chopped parsley
1 tablespoon grated Parmesan cheese

Heat the butter and oil in a pan. Add the garlic and onion and fry gently for 2–3 minutes. If the mushrooms are too large, cut into halves or quarters, otherwise leave whole. Add to the pan and fry gently for about 5 minutes, stirring frequently. Season well with salt and pepper. Spoon into warmed individual dishes and sprinkle each with a mixture of the parsley and Parmesan cheese. Serve hot with Melba toast.

Serves 4

Ratatouille

METRIC/IMPERIAL/AMERICAN
1 large onion, sliced
2 cloves garlic, crushed
25 g/1 oz/2 tablespoons butter
2 tablespoons/2 tablespoons/3 tablespoons oil
1 large aubergine, roughly chopped
2 courgettes, trimmed and sliced
1 small red or green pepper, deseeded and sliced
4 tomatoes, peeled and roughly chopped
salt and pepper
dash Worcestershire sauce
2 tablespoons/2 tablespoons/3 tablespoons water
chopped parsley to garnish

Fry the onion and garlic until soft in a mixture of the butter and oil. Add the aubergine, courgettes, pepper and tomatoes. Mix well and cook gently for 5–10 minutes, stirring frequently. Add the seasoning, Worcestershire sauce and water.

Cover the pan and simmer very gently for 45 minutes–1 hour, stirring occasionally. Adjust the seasoning, cool and chill. Serve on individual plates and garnish with parsley.
Note: The ratatouille may also be served hot.

Serves 4

Leek and pineapple cocktails

METRIC/IMPERIAL/AMERICAN
2 medium young leeks
4 rings canned pineapple, chopped
1 tablespoon finely chopped onion
4–6 tablespoons/4–6 tablespoons/$\frac{1}{3}$–$\frac{1}{2}$ cup French dressing
salt and pepper
100 g/4 oz/$\frac{1}{2}$ cup streaky bacon rashers, derinded and chopped

Trim the coarse green parts and root from the leeks, then finely slice the remainder. Wash very thoroughly. Blanch in boiling water for 2 minutes, rinse in cold water and drain very thoroughly. Add the pineapple, onion, dressing and seasoning. Toss well and leave to stand for 15 minutes.

Meanwhile, fry the bacon in its own fat until crispy, drain well and cool. Just before serving, sprinkle with the bacon and serve with hot crusty bread and parsley butter.

Serves 4

Avocado mousse

METRIC/IMPERIAL/AMERICAN
2 ripe avocados
75 g/3 oz/6 tablespoons soft cream cheese (Philadelphia)
1 clove garlic, crushed (optional)
4 tablespoons/4 tablespoons/$\frac{1}{3}$ cup single cream or top of the milk
1 teaspoon lemon juice
salt and pepper
1 teaspoon powdered gelatine
1 tablespoon water
watercress sprigs to garnish

Halve the avocados, remove the stones and peel. Mash the flesh until smooth. Beat in the softened cream cheese until completely blended then add the garlic, cream, lemon juice and seasoning to taste.

Dissolve the gelatine in the water in a basin over a pan of hot water, stir this evenly into the avocado mixture. Spoon into 4 individual dishes and chill for up to 2 hours until set. (Do not leave longer or the mousse may begin to discolour.) Garnish with the watercress and serve with toast.

Serves 4

Jellied tomato ring

METRIC/IMPERIAL/AMERICAN
600 ml/1 pint/2½ cups tomato juice
3 tablespoons/3 tablespoons/¼ cup wine vinegar
1 teaspoon Worcestershire sauce
1 tablespoon finely chopped onion
1 tablespoon powdered gelatine
350 g/12 oz/2 cups tomatoes, peeled, deseeded and
    chopped
GARNISH:
watercress
slices of stuffed olive

Blend the tomato juice with the vinegar, Worcestershire sauce
and onion. Dissolve the gelatine in 3 tablespoons/3 table-
spoons/¼ cup of the tomato liquid in a basin over a pan of hot
water. Return to the rest of the liquid, mix well and add the
chopped tomatoes. Turn into a 1-litre/1½-pint/2-pint ring
mould or six 150-ml/¼-pint/⅔-cup individual ring moulds and
chill until set. To serve, turn out and garnish the centre with
watercress and place slices of olive on the ring.

Serves 6

Mushrooms à la grecque

METRIC/IMPERIAL/AMERICAN
1 onion, chopped
2 carrots, diced
3 tablespoons/3 tablespoons/¼ cup oil
150 ml/¼ pint/⅔ cup dry white wine
1 bay leaf
1 clove garlic, crushed
salt and pepper
350 g/12 oz/3 cups button mushrooms
225 g/8 oz/½ lb tomatoes, peeled
chopped parsley to garnish

Sauté the onion and carrot in the oil until soft but not coloured.
Add the wine, bay leaf, garlic and seasoning, and bring to the
boil. Trim the mushrooms and halve or quarter if too large;
then add to the pan. Cover and cook gently for 5–6 minutes.
    Cut the tomatoes into quarters and remove the seeds.
Remove the pan from the heat, take out the bay leaf and add the
tomatoes. Cool then chill thoroughly. Serve in small shallow
dishes and sprinkle with the chopped parsley.

Serves 4

Melon and black grape cocktail

METRIC/IMPERIAL/AMERICAN
225 g/8 oz/½ lb black grapes
1 melon, firm but ripe
fresh mint leaves (optional)
egg white
1 tablespoon castor sugar
mint sprigs to garnish

Halve and depip the grapes, and place in a bowl. Cut the melon in half or quarters and remove the seeds. Either using a melon baller, scoop out as many melon balls as possible and add to the grapes with any juice; or cut the melon flesh into neat cubes. Crush a few mint leaves and mix into the fruit, if liked. Chill.

Before serving, dip the rims of 4 serving glasses into lightly beaten egg white then into castor sugar to give a frosted effect. Spoon in the melon and grape cocktail and garnish with mint sprigs.
Note: Fresh mint leaves or sprigs can also be given a frosted effect by dipping first into egg white and then castor sugar.

Serves 4

Ham and asparagus rolls

METRIC/IMPERIAL/AMERICAN
1 (227-g/8-oz/½-lb) packet frozen asparagus
salt
150 ml/¼ pint/⅔ cup thick mayonnaise
1–2 cloves garlic, crushed
1–2 tablespoons/1–2 tablespoons/1–3 tablespoons top of the milk
½ teaspoon grated lemon rind (optional)
6 slices cooked ham
paprika to garnish

Cook the asparagus in salted water until tender, drain and cool. Combine the mayonnaise, garlic to taste, sufficient top of the milk to give a coating consistency and lemon rind, if used.

Divide the asparagus between the slices of ham and roll up. Put the ham rolls on a serving dish or 6 small plates. Spoon the mayonnaise mixture over the ham and sprinkle with paprika. Serve with brown bread and butter.

Serves 6

Courgettes provençal

METRIC/IMPERIAL/AMERICAN
1 large onion, thinly sliced
1 clove garlic, crushed
50 g/2 oz/$\frac{1}{4}$ cup butter
0.5 kg/1 lb/1 lb courgettes, trimmed
350 g/12 oz/$\frac{3}{4}$ lb tomatoes, peeled and sliced
1 tablespoon tomato purée
salt and pepper
2 tablespoons/2 tablespoons/3 tablespoons water
2–3 tablespoons/2–3 tablespoons/3–4 tablespoons double
    cream
50 g/2 oz/$\frac{1}{2}$ cup Cheddar cheese, grated
25 g/1 oz/$\frac{1}{2}$ cup fresh breadcrumbs

Fry the onion and garlic in the butter until soft. Slice the courgettes and add to the onion mixture. Cook gently for 10 minutes, stirring occasionally. Add the tomatoes, tomato purée, seasoning and water. Cook gently for 10–15 minutes, stirring occasionally. Adjust the seasoning and stir in the cream.

   Spoon into one large or 6 small ovenproof dishes. Combine the cheese and breadcrumbs, and sprinkle over the courgette mixture. Place under a moderate grill until golden brown. Serve hot with granary bread and butter, if liked.

Serves 6

Spinach tartlets

METRIC/IMPERIAL/AMERICAN
100 g/4 oz/1 cup plain flour
salt and pepper
25 g/1 oz/2 tablespoons margarine
25 g/1 oz/2 tablespoons lard or white fat
225 g/8 oz/1 cup cooked spinach, chopped
$\frac{1}{4}$ teaspoon ground nutmeg
1 large egg, beaten
3 tablespoons/3 tablespoons/$\frac{1}{4}$ cup single cream
75 g/3 oz/$\frac{3}{4}$ cup mature Cheddar cheese, grated
slices of tomato to garnish

Sieve the flour into a bowl with a pinch of salt. Rub in the fats until the mixture resembles fine breadcrumbs. Add sufficient water to mix to a pliable dough. Roll out the dough and use to line 4 individual Yorkshire pudding or fluted flan tins.

   Combine the spinach, nutmeg, egg, cream, cheese and plenty of seasoning. Spoon into the uncooked pastry cases. Bake in a moderately hot oven (200°C, 400°F, Gas Mark 6) for about 30 minutes, until firm to the touch and the pastry is cooked through. Serve hot, warm or cold. Garnish with sliced tomatoes, cut into quarters.

Serves 4

Baked mushrooms

METRIC/IMPERIAL/AMERICAN
4 very large flat mushrooms (or 8 medium)
150 ml/¼ pint/⅔ cup stock
1 small onion, finely chopped
50 g/2 oz/¼ cup bacon, derinded and finely chopped
25 g/1 oz/2 tablespoons butter
225 g/8 oz/1 cup cottage cheese
salt and pepper
1 teaspoon dried oregano
parsley sprigs to garnish

Trim the stalks of the mushrooms then dip each mushroom in boiling stock for ½–1 minute. Drain and place on a grill rack, stem upwards.

Fry the onion and bacon in the butter until golden brown. Cool slightly, then mix into the cottage cheese with the seasoning and oregano. Almost cover the dark surface of the mushrooms with the cheese mixture. Place under a moderate grill for about 5 minutes or until the cheese is lightly tinged brown. Serve hot on a croûte of toast and garnish with the parsley.

Serves 4

Apple cocktails

METRIC/IMPERIAL/AMERICAN
2 large (or 4 small) green eating apples
3 tablespoons/3 tablespoons/¼ cup thick mayonnaise
1 tablespoon lemon juice
salt and pepper
good pinch curry powder
8 stuffed olives
50–75 g/2–3 oz/about ½ cup peeled prawns or shrimps
1 tablespoon chopped chives
50 g/2 oz/½ cup Cheddar cheese, finely diced
watercress sprigs to garnish

Cut the apples in half, scoop out the flesh and core, leaving a firm shell inside the peel. (If using whole apples, cut a slice off the top and then scoop out the flesh and core.)

Combine the mayonnaise, lemon juice, seasoning and curry powder. Remove the core from the apple flesh, chop the remaining flesh and add to the mayonnaise together with the sliced olives, halved prawns, chives and cheese. Mix thoroughly then spoon back into the apple shells. Arrange on small plates, garnish with the watercress and serve at once.

Serves 4

Fish starters

These starters make a welcome change and you will see from the recipes in this chapter that prawn cocktail is not the only fish starter! A variety of frozen fish is available and this is a good buy particularly if you do not have a reliable wet fish shop in your area.

Smoked haddock mousse

METRIC/IMPERIAL/AMERICAN
350 g/12 oz/¾ lb smoked haddock fillet
about 150 ml/¼ pint/⅔ cup milk
25 g/1 oz/2 tablespoons butter
1 tablespoon flour
salt and pepper
good pinch ground mace
2 eggs, separated
1½ teaspoons powdered gelatine
1 tablespoon water
150 ml/¼ pint/⅔ cup soured cream
300 ml/½ pint/1¼ cups liquid aspic jelly
GARNISH:
slices of hard-boiled egg
parsley sprigs

Cook the fish in the milk until tender. Drain, reserving 150 ml/¼ pint/⅔ cup cooking liquor, made up with more milk if necessary. Cool the fish, remove skin and bones, and flake.

Melt the butter in a pan, stir in the flour and cook for 1 minute then gradually add the reserved milk. Bring to the boil for 1 minute then add salt, pepper and mace. Beat in yolks.

Dissolve the gelatine in the water in a basin over a pan of hot water. Stir into the sauce, then add the soured cream. Add the fish and mix thoroughly. Whisk the egg whites until stiff and fold into the mixture. Pour into a large or 6 individual dishes and chill until set. Pour a layer of liquid aspic over the surface and leave to set. Garnish with the egg slices and parsley.

Serves 6

Sardine-stuffed lemons

METRIC/IMPERIAL/AMERICAN
4 lemons
2 tablespoons/2 tablespoons/3 tablespoons soured cream
1 (120-g/4¼-oz/4¼-oz) can sardines, drained and mashed
2 tablespoons/2 tablespoons/3 tablespoons finely chopped
   cucumber
1 tablespoon chopped capers
salt and pepper
dash Tabasco sauce
1 small lettuce

Cut the tops off the lemons and a small piece from the base so
they stand firmly. Scoop out the lemon flesh and squeeze
1 tablespoon juice from the flesh.

Mix together the soured cream, lemon juice, mashed
sardines, cucumber and capers. Season to taste with salt, pepper
and Tabasco. Spoon the mixture into the lemon shells, chill
thoroughly and serve on lettuce leaves with fingers of toast.

Serves 4

Tuna creams

METRIC/IMPERIAL/AMERICAN
150 ml/¼ pint/⅔ cup natural yogurt
4 tablespoons/4 tablespoons/⅓ cup thick mayonnaise
1 tablespoon lemon juice
salt and pepper
2 teaspoons powdered gelatine
2 tablespoons/2 tablespoons/3 tablespoons water
4 spring onions, finely sliced
1 hard-boiled egg, chopped
2 gherkins, chopped
1 tablespoon capers, chopped
1 (198-g/7-oz/7-oz) can tuna, drained and flaked
GARNISH:
slices of cucumber
slices of lemon

Combine the yogurt, mayonnaise and lemon juice, and season
well. Dissolve the gelatine in the water in a basin over a pan of
hot water. Stir into the yogurt mixture.

Mix together the onions, hard-boiled egg, gherkins, capers
and tuna, and fold into the yogurt mixture. Spoon into
4 individual dishes and chill until set. Serve garnished with a
twist of cucumber and lemon.

Serves 4

Taramasalata

METRIC/IMPERIAL/AMERICAN
175–225 g/6–8 oz/⅓–½ lb smoked cod's roe
3 slices white bread
1 teaspoon finely chopped onion
1–2 cloves garlic, crushed
about 4 tablespoons/4 tablespoons/⅓ cup oil
juice of 1 lemon
2 teaspoons chopped parsley
salt and black pepper
1 small lettuce
GARNISH:
watercress sprigs
black olives

Remove and discard the skin from the cod's roe, mash until smooth. Remove the crusts from the bread then soak in cold water; squeeze almost dry and crumble into the cod's roe. Add the onion and garlic, and pound to a paste. Gradually beat in sufficient oil and lemon juice until the mixture becomes thick and creamy. Beat in the chopped parsley and season to taste. Place the taramasalata on lettuce leaves and garnish with watercress sprigs and black olives. Serve with fingers of hot toast and butter.

Serves 4

Chalford cocktail

METRIC/IMPERIAL/AMERICAN
2 avocados
2 grapefruit
2 tablespoons/2 tablespoons/3 tablespoons thick
　mayonnaise
1 tablespoon tomato ketchup
1 tablespoon cream
dash Tabasco sauce
dash Worcestershire sauce
salt and pepper
100 g/4 oz/⅔ cup peeled prawns
twists of cucumber to garnish

Halve the avocados and remove the stones. Prepare the grapefruit segments as for Victorian cocktail (see page 39). Rub the cut surface of the avocados with grapefruit juice.

Combine the mayonnaise, ketchup, cream, Tabasco, Worcestershire sauce and seasoning. Fold in the prawns and grapefruit segments, spoon into the avocado stone cavities. Garnish with the twists of cucumber.

Serves 4

Creamed scallops

METRIC/IMPERIAL/AMERICAN
6 scallops
150 ml/¼ pint/⅔ cup dry white wine
150 ml/¼ pint/⅔ cup water
½ teaspoon grated lemon rind
1 tablespoon lemon juice
salt and pepper
25 g/1 oz/2 tablespoons butter
1 onion, finely chopped
2 tablespoons/2 tablespoons/3 tablespoons flour
4 tablespoons/4 tablespoons/⅓ cup cream
40 g/1½ oz/¾ cup fresh breadcrumbs
40 g/1½ oz/3 tablespoons Cheddar cheese, finely grated
watercress to garnish

Loosen the scallops from their shells and wash well. Cut the flesh into cubes and place in a saucepan with the wine, water, lemon rind and juice, and seasoning. Bring to the boil, cover and simmer for 10 minutes until the scallops are tender. Strain and reserve 200 ml/⅓ pint/¾ cup cooking liquor for the sauce.

Melt the butter and sauté the onion until soft. Stir in the flour and cook for 1 minute. Gradually add the cooking liquor and bring to the boil. Season, replace the scallops and simmer for 2 minutes. Remove from the heat, stir in the cream and spoon into 4 deep scallop shells or individual flameproof dishes. Sprinkle with a mixture of the breadcrumbs and cheese, and brown under a moderate grill. Garnish with watercress and serve with brown bread and butter.

Serves 4

Smoked trout mousse

METRIC/IMPERIAL/AMERICAN
15 g/½ oz/1 tablespoon butter
15 g/½ oz/2 tablespoons flour
150 ml/¼ pint/⅔ cup milk
salt and pepper
150 ml/¼ pint/⅔ cup soured cream
1 tablespoon lemon juice
½ teaspoon creamed horseradish
1 (175–225 g/6–8 oz/6–8 oz) smoked trout
1½ teaspoons powdered gelatine
1½ tablespoons/1½ tablespoons/2 tablespoons water
GARNISH:
slices of tomato
lemon butterflies
mustard and cress

Melt the butter in a pan, stir in the flour and cook for 1 minute. Gradually add the milk and bring to the boil. Simmer for 2 minutes, stirring. Remove from the heat, season to taste and beat in the soured cream, lemon juice and horseradish.

Remove the skin and bones from the trout and either mash very finely and mix into the sauce or place the fish and sauce in a liquidiser and blend until smooth.

Dissolve the gelatine in the water in a small basin over hot water, then stir evenly into the mousse. Pour into 4 individual ramekin dishes, a larger dish or into a lightly greased small mould and chill until set. Garnish with the tomato slices, lemon butterflies and mustard and cress.

Serves 4

53

Marinated kipper fillets

METRIC/IMPERIAL/AMERICAN
175 g/6 oz/6 oz frozen kipper fillets in a boilable bag
2 tablespoons/2 tablespoons/3 tablespoons wine vinegar
2 tablespoons/2 tablespoons/3 tablespoons oil
1 tablespoon lemon juice
salt and pepper
pinch garlic powder
1 small onion, finely sliced
parsley sprigs to garnish

Put the kippers in the bag in a pan of cold water. Bring to the boil and simmer for 2 minutes only. Remove from the water and turn the kippers into a shallow dish.

Combine the vinegar, oil, lemon juice, seasoning and garlic powder, and pour over kippers. Add the onion and allow to become cold. Turn the kippers occasionally, then cover and chill for 12–24 hours. Serve pieces of drained kipper on individual plates with a few pieces of the onion on top and garnished with parsley. Serve with brown bread and butter.

Serves 3–4

Danish style herring salad

METRIC/IMPERIAL/AMERICAN
1 tablespoon tomato purée
2 tablespoons/2 tablespoons/3 tablespoons tomato
  ketchup
2 tablespoons/2 tablespoons/3 tablespoons wine vinegar
1 teaspoon French mustard
good dash Worcestershire sauce
1 tablespoon lemon juice
salt and black pepper
4 pickled herrings, drained
1 onion, finely chopped
mustard and cress to garnish

Whisk together the tomato purée, ketchup, vinegar, mustard, Worcestershire sauce, lemon juice and seasoning. Slice the herrings thickly and arrange rolled up in 4 small bowls or a larger dish, scattering the chopped onion over. Spoon the tomato mixture over the fish, cover and chill for several hours or preferably overnight. Garnish with mustard and cress.

Serves 4

Moules marinière

METRIC/IMPERIAL/AMERICAN
about 3.5 litres/6 pints/7 pints fresh mussels
50 g/2 oz/¼ cup butter
1 medium onion, very finely chopped
½ bottle dry white wine
bouquet garni
salt and pepper
2 teaspoons flour
chopped parsley to garnish

Thoroughly wash and scrub the mussels, removing any
barnacles, mud, etc. Discard any which do not close when given
a sharp tap.

Melt 40 g/1½ oz/3 tablespoons of the butter in a pan and sauté
the onion until soft but not coloured. Add the wine, bouquet
garni and seasoning. Cover and simmer gently for 5 minutes.
Add the mussels a few at a time, cover the pan and simmer
gently for about 5 minutes, shaking the pan frequently until all
the mussels are open.

Place the mussels in soup bowls and keep warm. Cream the
remaining butter with the flour and whisk into the juices,
discarding the bouquet garni. Bring to the boil for 3–4 minutes,
adjust the seasoning and pour over the mussels. Sprinkle with
the parsley and serve with plenty of hot crusty French bread.

Serves 4–6

Crab au gratin

METRIC/IMPERIAL/AMERICAN
225 g/8 oz/½ lb crabmeat
40 g/1½ oz/3 tablespoons butter
1 small onion, finely chopped
25 g/1 oz/¼ cup flour
300 ml/½ pint/1¼ cups milk
salt and pepper
½ teaspoon made mustard
good dash Worcestershire sauce
2 teaspoons lemon juice
25 g/1 oz/½ cup fresh breadcrumbs
50 g/2 oz/½ cup Cheddar cheese, finely grated
paprika
GARNISH:
parsley sprigs
slices of lemon

Flake the crabmeat. If using fresh crab, remove all the meat –
brown and white – from the shell and claws.

Melt the butter and fry the onion until soft. Stir in the flour
and cook for 1 minute. Add the milk and bring to the boil. Stir
in the seasoning, mustard, Worcestershire sauce and lemon
juice, and simmer for 2 minutes. Add the crabmeat and heat
through thoroughly. Spoon into 4–6 small flameproof dishes or
scallop shells. Mix the breadcrumbs with the cheese and a good
shake of paprika and spoon over the crab mixture. Place under a
moderate grill until the topping is well browned. Garnish with
the parsley and quartered lemon slices.

Serves 4–6

Prawns Newburg

METRIC/IMPERIAL/AMERICAN
1 small onion, finely chopped
50 g/2 oz/¼ cup butter
225 g/8 oz/1⅓ cups peeled prawns
2 tablespoons/2 tablespoons/3 tablespoons lemon juice
4 tablespoons/4 tablespoons/⅓ cup sherry or Madeira
salt and pepper
50 g/2 oz/¼ cup long-grain rice, cooked
2 egg yolks
150 ml/¼ pint/⅔ cup single cream
watercress sprigs to garnish

Fry the onion gently in the butter until soft. Add the prawns and cook gently for 5 minutes, shaking frequently. Add the lemon juice, sherry, seasoning and bring to the boil. Add the cooked rice and mix thoroughly.

Beat the egg yolks into the cream and add to the pan. Heat gently, stirring continuously, until just below boiling point. Adjust the seasoning and serve in small dishes. Garnish with the watercress and serve with hot toast.

Serves 4

Baked avocados with crab

METRIC/IMPERIAL/AMERICAN
25 g/1 oz/2 tablespoons butter
1 small onion, finely chopped
100–150 g/4–5 oz/4–5 oz crabmeat
2 tablespoons/2 tablespoons/3 tablespoons fresh
   breadcrumbs
1–2 tablespoons/1–2 tablespoons/1–3 tablespoons cream
salt and pepper
paprika
2 ripe avocados
25 g/1 oz/¼ cup Emmenthal or Cheddar cheese, finely
   grated
parsley sprigs to garnish

Melt the butter in a pan and fry the onion until soft. Add the crabmeat and cook gently for 3–4 minutes, stirring frequently. Stir in the breadcrumbs, cream and season with salt, pepper and paprika.

Halve the avocados and remove the stones. Stand the halves in an ovenproof dish. Spoon the crab mixture into the stone cavities. Sprinkle with the cheese and bake in a moderately hot oven (200°C, 400°F, Gas Mark 6) for 15–20 minutes. Serve hot, garnished with parsley.

Serves 4

Egg and cheese starters

Eggs and cheese are excellent sources of protein which is most important in our daily diet. They make nutritious starters which may also be served when the family want a quick and tasty snack. Stuffed egg mayonnaise is easy to prepare and although surprise cheese soufflés need a little more attention they make an impressive starter to any meal.

Baked eggs

METRIC/IMPERIAL/AMERICAN
100 g/4 oz/½ cup lean bacon rashers, derinded and chopped
50 g/2 oz/½ cup button mushrooms, chopped
15 g/½ oz/1 tablespoon butter
salt and black pepper
4 eggs
150 ml/¼ pint/⅔ cup single or double cream
gherkin fans to garnish

Fry the bacon and mushrooms in the melted butter until the bacon is cooked. Season well with pepper and a little salt. Spoon into the base of 4 lightly greased, individual ovenproof ramekin dishes. Carefully break an egg into each dish. Spoon 2 tablespoons/2 tablespoons/3 tablespoons cream over each egg and stand the dishes on a baking sheet. Bake in a hot oven (220°C, 425°F, Gas Mark 7) for 12–15 minutes until the egg is just set. Garnish with a gherkin fan and serve with crispbread and butter.
Note: Peeled and thinly sliced tomatoes can be used in place of the bacon and mushrooms for a change.

Serves 4

Surprise cheese soufflés

METRIC/IMPERIAL/AMERICAN
50 g/2 oz/¼ cup lean bacon, derinded and chopped
100 g/4 oz/1 cup mushrooms, chopped
50 g/2 oz/¼ cup butter
salt and pepper
25 g/1 oz/¼ cup flour
200 ml/⅓ pint/¾ cup milk
½ teaspoon oregano
¼ teaspoon made mustard
2 eggs, separated
50 g/2 oz/½ cup mature Cheddar cheese, finely grated

Fry the bacon and mushrooms in half the butter until soft. Season. Spoon into the bases of 6 individual soufflé dishes and stand them on a baking sheet.

Melt the remaining butter in a pan. Stir in the flour and cook for 1 minute. Gradually add the milk and bring to the boil. Add the oregano, mustard, seasoning and egg yolks. Simmer for 2 minutes, stirring. Remove from the heat and beat in the cheese until melted. Cool slightly. Stiffly whisk the egg whites and fold evenly into the sauce. Spoon into the dishes. Bake in a moderately hot oven (200°C, 400°F, Gas Mark 6) for about 20 minutes or until well risen and golden brown. Serve immediately.

Serves 6

Chackchouka

METRIC/IMPERIAL/AMERICAN
25 g/1 oz/2 tablespoons butter
3 tablespoons/3 tablespoons/¼ cup oil
3 onions, sliced
0.5 kg/1 lb/1 lb tomatoes, peeled and sliced
1 red pepper, deseeded and sliced
1 green pepper, deseeded and sliced
salt and pepper
6 eggs

Heat the butter and oil in a saucepan, add the onions and fry until soft. Stir in the tomatoes and peppers, cover and simmer gently for about 10 minutes. Season well and place in a shallow ovenproof dish or 6 individual ovenproof dishes. Make wells in the mixture and break an egg into each. Cook in a hot oven (220°C, 425°F, Gas Mark 7) for 10–15 minutes until set. Serve hot.

Serves 6

Cottage cheese pâté

METRIC/IMPERIAL/AMERICAN
2 sticks celery, finely chopped
40 g/1½ oz/⅓ cup shelled walnuts, chopped
1 tablespoon finely chopped onion
1 tablespoon chopped chives
salt and black pepper
good dash Worcestershire sauce
1 clove garlic, crushed
225 g/8 oz/1 cup cottage cheese
40 g/1½ oz/3 tablespoons butter, melted

Put the celery, walnuts, onion, chives, seasoning, Worcester-shire sauce, garlic and cottage cheese into a bowl and mix very well, breaking down the cottage cheese. Add the butter and mix in evenly. Spoon into a large dish or 4 small serving dishes. Chill until firm.

Serves 4

Stuffed egg mayonnaise

METRIC/IMPERIAL/AMERICAN
6 hard-boiled eggs
150 ml/¼ pint/⅔ cup thick mayonnaise
1 teaspoon curry powder
salt and pepper
2 teaspoons chopped capers
1 small lettuce
lemon juice
1 (190-g/6½-oz/6½-oz) can pimientos, drained, to garnish

Halve the eggs lengthways, scoop out the yolks and mash thoroughly. Add 1 tablespoon mayonnaise, half the curry powder, seasoning and capers. Spoon back into the egg white halves.

Arrange lettuce on 6 small plates, place 2 egg halves on each, cut side downwards. Beat the remaining curry powder into the mayonnaise, with sufficient lemon juice to give a coating consistency. Spoon over the eggs until completely coated. Cut the pimientos into narrow strips and use to garnish the eggs.
Note: The curry powder can be omitted, if preferred.

Serves 6

Celebration starters

When you are serving a special occasion meal, an exciting new starter will certainly impress your guests. The recipes in this chapter have been created with that in mind, yet do not necessitate the hostess spending hours in the kitchen.

Seafood bouchées

METRIC/IMPERIAL/AMERICAN
1 (369-g/13-oz/13-oz) packet frozen puff pastry, thawed
beaten egg to glaze
40 g/1½ oz/3 tablespoons butter
1 tablespoon finely chopped onion
25 g/1 oz/¼ cup flour
150 ml/¼ pint/⅔ cup milk
4 tablespoons/4 tablespoons/⅓ cup double cream
salt and pepper
100 g/4 oz/⅔ cup peeled prawns
50 g/2 oz/2 oz smoked salmon pieces
1 (170-g/6-oz/6-oz) jar mussels, drained and chopped

Roll out the pastry to 0.5-cm/¼-inch thickness and cut into about ten 5–7.5-cm/2–3-inch plain rounds. Place on a baking sheet and brush with beaten egg. Using a 2.5-cm/1-inch plain round cutter, mark a circle in the centre of each. Chill for 10 minutes then bake in a hot oven (230°C, 450°F, Gas Mark 8) for 15–20 minutes until well risen and golden brown. Transfer to a wire rack and remove the lids and centres.

Melt the butter in a pan and sauté the onion until soft. Stir in the flour, cook for 1 minute then add the milk. Simmer for 2 minutes then beat in the cream and seasoning. Add the prawns, salmon and mussels, and heat. Spoon into the bouchées. Replace the lids and reheat in a moderate oven for about 10 minutes.

Serves 10–12

Salmon mousses

METRIC/IMPERIAL/AMERICAN
25 g/1 oz/2 tablespoons butter
25 g/1 oz/¼ cup flour
about 300 ml/½ pint/1¼ cups milk
¼ teaspoon dry mustard
salt and pepper
1 tablespoon wine vinegar
3 large eggs, separated
300–350 g/10–12 oz/10–12 oz cooked salmon
150 ml/¼ pint/⅔ cup single cream
4 teaspoons powdered gelatine
3 tablespoons/3 tablespoons/¼ cup water
slices of cucumber
slices of stuffed olive
150 ml/¼ pint/⅔ cup liquid aspic jelly

Melt the butter in a pan, stir in the flour and cook for 1 minute. Add the milk and bring to the boil, stirring. Add the mustard, seasoning and vinegar. Simmer gently for 2 minutes, stirring. Beat in the egg yolks and cook for 1 minute.

Skin, bone and flake the salmon. Add to the mixture with the cream. Dissolve the gelatine in the water in a basin over a pan of hot water. Cool slightly then stir into the salmon mixture. Leave until beginning to set then whisk the egg whites stiffly and fold in. Pour into 8 individual ramekin dishes and chill until set. Place cucumber and olive slices on the mousses, then cover with a layer of the jelly. Chill.

Serves 8

Smoked salmon and asparagus quiches

METRIC/IMPERIAL/AMERICAN
225 g/8 oz/2 cups plain flour
salt and pepper
50 g/2 oz/¼ cup margarine
50 g/2 oz/¼ cup lard or white fat
225 g/8 oz/½ lb frozen asparagus, cooked
175 g/6 oz/6 oz smoked salmon pieces
4 eggs
450 ml/¾ pint/2 cups single cream

Sieve the flour with a pinch of salt and rub in the fats until the mixture resembles fine breadcrumbs. Add sufficient cold water to mix to a pliable dough. Wrap in foil and chill for 30 minutes. Roll out the dough and use to line a 25-cm/10-inch fluted flan tin or six or eight 11-cm/4½-inch individual flan cases.

Roughly chop the asparagus and place in the bottom of the uncooked pastry case or cases. Cut the salmon into narrow strips and arrange over the asparagus. Beat the eggs with the seasoning and cream, and spoon over the salmon. Cook in a hot oven (220°C, 425°F, Gas Mark 7) for 10–15 minutes then reduce to 180°C, 350°F, Gas Mark 4 for a further 30–40 minutes for a large quiche or 20–25 minutes for the small quiches until just set and lightly browned. Serve warm.
Note: Well-drained canned or cooked fresh asparagus can be used in place of the frozen variety.

Serves 6–8

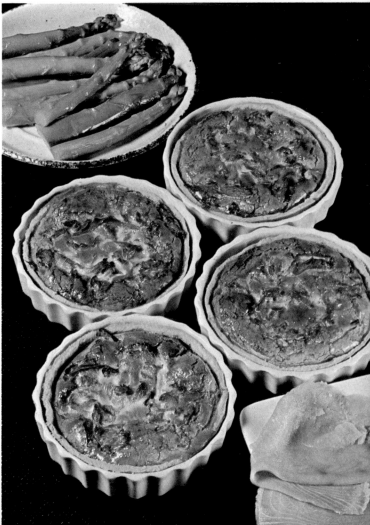

Ham and pâté cornets

METRIC/IMPERIAL/AMERICAN
6 large thin slices cooked ham
50 g/2 oz/¼ cup butter
225 g/8 oz/½ lb soft smooth pâté
1–2 tablespoons/1–2 tablespoons/1–3 tablespoons double
   cream
salt and pepper
1 clove garlic, crushed (optional)
300 ml/½ pint/1¼ cups liquid aspic jelly
GARNISH:
black olives
mustard and cress

Cut each slice of ham in half diagonally (or use 12 small slices). Roll each piece round a cream horn tin and press lightly into another tin. Roll the ham around this tin and place in another. Continue in this way until all the ham is used, to keep in shape. Wrap lightly in polythene and chill for 15–20 minutes.

Cream the butter until soft then beat in the pâté and sufficient cream to give a piping consistency. Season with salt and pepper and add the garlic, if liked. Place in a piping bag fitted with a star nozzle. Carefully remove the ham cornets from the tins, one at a time, and fill with the piped pâté. Place on a wire rack and chill again. Leave the aspic jelly until on the point of setting and then spoon over the cornets. Garnish each with a piece of black olive and chill until set. Serve with fingers of toast and garnish with mustard and cress.

Serves 6–12

Hors d'oeuvre

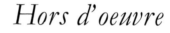

Arrange each salad separately in a small dish and serve them all together, allowing everyone to help themselves.
(a) Tomato salad: Arrange 225 g/8 oz/½ lb sliced tomatoes in a dish. Combine 3 tablespoons/3 tablespoons/¼ cup soured cream and 1 tablespoon lemon juice with salt and pepper, and spoon over the tomatoes. Sprinkle with chopped chives.
(b) Cucumber and corn salad: Combine a 10-cm/4-inch piece cucumber, diced, 1 small sliced onion and 1 (198-g/7-oz/7-oz) can sweetcorn; add 2–3 tablespoons/2–3 tablespoons/3–4 tablespoons French dressing and seasoning, and toss well. Put into a dish and arrange canned sardines around the edge.
(c) Mixed meat salad: Arrange overlapping slices of liver sausage, salami and garlic sausage (100 g/4 oz/¼ lb each meat) on a dish and garnish with parsley.
(d) Egg mayonnaise: Cut 4 hard-boiled eggs into quarters and arrange on a bed of shredded lettuce in a dish. Combine 4 tablespoons/4 tablespoons/⅓ cup mayonnaise, ¼ teaspoon curry powder and seasoning, and add sufficient lemon juice to give a coating consistency. Spoon over the eggs and garnish with a lattice of anchovy fillets with sliced stuffed olives.
(e) Beetroot and carrot salad: Combine 175 g/6 oz/1 cup finely diced beetroot and 2 grated carrots. Add 2–3 tablespoons/2–3 tablespoons/3–4 tablespoons French dressing and seasoning. Spoon into a dish and sprinkle with chopped parsley.

Serves 8